BEST FRIENDS

By the same Author

Lunchtime Concert
The Inhabitants
Coda
The Gymnasium
The Technicians
Stay Where You Are
Jack The Giant-Killer
Neither Here Nor There

PLAYSCRIPT 106

BEST FRIENDS
The Committee
The Twenty-Second Day

Olwen Wymark

JOHN CALDER · LONDON
RIVERRUN PRESS · NEW YORK

Best Friends and Other Plays first published in Great Britain, 1984, by
John Calder (Publishers) Ltd.,
18 Brewer Street, London W1R 4AS

and in USA, 1984, by
Riverrun Press,
175 Fifth Avenue, New York, NY 10010

British Library Cataloguing in Publication Data
Wymark, Olwen
  Best Friends.—(Playscripts; 106)
  I. Title   II. Series
  822'.914   PR6073.Y/

ISBN 0-7145-3955-4

SUBSIDISED BY THE
Arts Council
OF GREAT BRITAIN

Typeset in 9/10pt Times Roman by Acorn Origination, Bournemouth.
Printed and bound in Great Britain by Hillman Printers, Frome, Somerset.

CONTENTS

Best Friends   *1*

The Committee   *45*

The Twenty-Second Day   *55*

BEST FRIENDS
The Committee
The Twenty-Second Day

Characters

BABA
JOE
NELLY
GINGER
STANLEY
RAYMOND

Written for the BBC Radio Theatre 81 and for the Richmond Orange Tree Theatre in March 1981, transmitted on Radio 3 in April.

BABA	Ruth Goring
NELLY	Ann Windsor
JOE/ELI	Christopher Hancock
RAYMOND	Dominic Letts
GINGER	Madeline Church

Directed for the stage by Sam Walter and for the radio by Richard Wortley.

ACT ONE

Music is playing as the audience is coming in. The first movement of the Dvorak Cello Concerto. The stage is bare except for a writing-table and a chair and a stool nearby with some papers and books on it. On the table a bowl with grapes and pomegranates in it, some flowers in a small vase, a couple of shells and rocks. There is a brightly coloured cushion on the chair. One lamp is on, if possible hanging some several feet above the table and making a circle of light for the first scene of the play. When the play begins all the lights go out except the lamp which dims to low and the music fades out to silence. After a pause, the second movement of the Concerto starts (quite loud to differentiate it from the level it was playing before the play began) and the lamp dims to black. In the blackout after the opening phrases, the music crossfades to being played in the distance on a cassette recorder offstage. In the blackout we hear footsteps and the music gradually getting louder. It is coming from a portable radio/recorder being carried by a woman, BABA. We hear her humming along to the music and when a very affecting passage is reached, her voice breaks.

BABA *(emotionally)*. I can't bear it. *(Pause. Then irritable.)* Oh be quiet!

She switches the music off and the lights come up immediately to the circle of light from the lamp. BABA is in her forties. She's wearing a rather ethnic looking dressing-gown and she is carrying, in addition to the recorder, a fairly big notebook, cigarettes, matches, an ashtray and a pen. She moves to the table and begins to speak again in a moderately exaggerated emotional tone.

BABA. The music rose to a kind of terrible poignancy. Caught and suddenly unbearably moved by the pain and sweetness of the sound, her eyes filled with tears. *(She puts the recorder down on the floor. Pause. Matter-of-factly to herself)* I **said** be quiet. *(She begins rather meticulously to arrange the things she's carrying on the table. As she does this she speaks to herself again, this time in a broadish Irish accent.)* Take my word for it all this blubbing over bits of music means nothing at all except you're a sentimental old bag. Simply self-indulgence and showing off I'm sorry to say. **And** there's nobody here to see how sensitive you are. Nobody at all. *(Then again to herself. Own accent. Irritable).* All right. *(She yawns and groans slightly. Stands looking at the table. Then rather briskly, she gets a Kleenex out of her pocket and polishes the ashtray very thoroughly. Puts it*

1

back down on the table. Conversational.) This ashtray actually ruins the
effect we are trying to achieve here, friends. Might the fact that it
completely spoils the look of my writing-table prove sufficient argument
to persuade me to give up smoking? Probably not, no. *(Pause. Then
resonantly)* 'My Writing Table.' *(Then as to TV camera in the tones of the
narrator of some pretentious literary documentary.)* Yes ladies and
gentlemen, Barbara Phillips' own writing table. There's something very
harmonious about it isn't there. Peaceful and yet at the same time . . .
stimulating. The bowl of grapes and pomegranates — a touch of Ancient
Greece here — the simple posy in the chipped Venetian glass, the few
seashells and stones sculpted and polished by the ocean . . . all these
random elements expressing in their own way the grace and power of her
work. Yes, at this very table Ms Phillips wrote all her famous plays.
(Confidential) I wonder how widely known it is that up until very recently
indeed, Barbara Phillips was an amateur writer! Hard to believe but
true. Until her meteoric rise to fame — *(breaks off, maddened with
herself)* All right! *(She sits in the chair. Slumps. Then reaches for a
cigarette. Stops. Imperative.)* And don't smoke. *(Pause.)* And don't just
sit there doing nothing either. Begin. *(Pause.)* I said begin. Just open the
notebook and start working on the play. Doesn't matter if it seems
terrible. It can be rewritten. Or thrown away. Just begin. *(Then in a rich
operatic contralto, she sings.)* Take up your biro and begin, we implore
you. *(Laughs. Pause. Then purposeful.)* Right. Get on!

*She opens the notebook and leafs through, pausing to glance at pages. Then
starts reading bits out loud to herself inaudibly at first. Then clearly.*

BABA.   Annie gets up and goes to the window. She looks at Eli. Annie:
How are you feeling now?

*Then she reads the following clearly and in unison with a man who has come
on from the side. This is JOE who is also Eli in Baba's play.*

BABA & JOE *(in unison)*.   As a matter of fact I'm feeling a great deal
better. *(During the following BABA gets up and turns to look at JOE as
he speaks.)*
JOE.   It might have something to do with the piano tuner. I'd been
dreading him . . . I mean, really dreading. I was absolutely infuriated
with you for asking me to be here when he came. *(Pained.)* You must
have known the piano being tuned could easily precipitate me into a total
nervous collapse. I thought you were being deliberately sadistic. *(Pause.
Looks at her.)* Were you, Annie? *(She is silent.)* Annie?
BABA *(laughs)*.   Oh Eli . . . *(Pause. Goodnatured.)* You'd like that
because it would cheer you up to believe that you and I have a
sado-masochistic relationship. I had to go and visit old Mrs Fisher in
hospital. *(Smiles at him.)* Would you rather have done that, Eli?
JOE.   No. *(Shudders.)* My God no.
BABA.   Well then. So how did the piano tuner make you feel better? He
is an extremely nice man.
JOE.   Yes he looked nice. Very benign. But I didn't actually talk to him at
all apart from hello and here's the piano. Then I retired rather rapidly up

to the attic. It seemed like a very good time to sort through those boxes of books. I thought I wouldn't be able to hear him up there. But perhaps sound travels up like heat. Distant but very, very clear. One note over and over again and then the next note. And then back to the first one. And then on. Over and over again. *(Pause. Thoughtful)* However, to my surprise I liked it. I found it entirely peaceful. Soothing. The sun was pouring through that little skylight up there and there were pigeons on the roof cooing and walking about and chuntering to each other. *(Pause. Smiles at her)* I put that old cane chair in the patch of sunlight and just sat there feeling really rather amazingly all right. I went to sleep. I haven't slept that well for weeks. I dreamed! *(Pause. Remembering)* I was swimming in the Great Salt Lake. There were a lot of sort of armadillo like things swimming with me. Very amiable and friendly toward me they all were. *(Pause. Surprised)* Come to think of it I may have been one myself. Yes, I probably was.

BABA *(friendly)*.   An armadillo in the attic. Somehow that's very like you. A metaphor to conjure you up.

JOE.   Very funny.

BABA.   I was being serious.

JOE.   You weren't. You were making one of your sadistic jokes. When I woke up it was dusk but it was still very warm. I felt as if I'd like to spend the rest of my life up there. But I was hungry so I came downstairs feeling very clear and calm. And then I had a row with the child.

BABA.   I know. I heard you.

JOE.   Heard? But you weren't anywhere in the house. I'd looked for you.

BABA.   I was in the garden. I was watering my seedlings under that window when you two started so I just stayed there and listened.

JOE.   Did you hear all of it?

BABA.   Yes.

JOE.   I've never been able to be that angry with him before.

BABA.   No.

JOE.   You do realise what I've done.

BABA.   Yes.

JOE.   Do you forgive me?

BABA.   What for?

JOE *(surprised)*.   For spilling the beans.

BABA *(laughs)*.   Oh Eli, the beans were spilled years ago. Eight . . . nine perhaps. By me.

JOE *(stares at her. A pause)*.   You never told me that!

BABA.   No. *(Another pause)*

JOE.   Revenge do you think?

BABA *(candid)*.   I don't know.

JOE *(after a longish pause. Chatty)*.   Tell you what's interesting about this. It's total confirmation that you are in charge here. The decision-maker, the programme planner, the boss. I suppose I've always known it but I pushed the thought away because it was so much more cosy to go on colluding in your little set-up. The myth that I was respected, looked up to, even given way to. My advice sought, my opinions esteemed . . . oh absolutely! The lord and master. The man of the house. *(Pause)* The fool of the house.

BABA.   Eli! Just because you need someone to blame for your frustration and your self hatred and your boring depression — yes I said boring! I honestly think you —

JOE *(interrupts)*. Stop. Wait. There's just one thing I'd like to say.

He goes to her and they stand face to face in silence. Then he walks offstage. BABA sits in the chair, her elbows on the table, head in hands. The circle of light widens and comes up to full stage lighting and we can see the room, just bare walls and the furniture as described at the beginning. A door upstage of centre through which only the 'real' characters enter. 'Play' characters come on from the side. NELLY, attractive, late forties, comes in the door and sits on the writing-table with her back to BABA during the light change. She has some typewritten pages in her hands. She finishes reading. She looks over at BABA.

NELLY.   So? What was he going to say, Baba?

BABA *(looks up)*.   I don't know. That's why I stopped.

NELLY *(flips through the pages)*. Well honestly! I'm amazed.

BABA *(nervous)*.   How do you mean? (NELLY *gets up. Waves the script at her.*)

NELLY.   You never told me anything about this.

BABA.   Well no, I — (NELLY *goes to the stool, takes the papers and books off it and sits with the script in her lap.*)

NELLY.   How long have you been doing this, Baba? Writing plays.

BABA.   Oh . . . about two years.

NELLY.   Why didn't you tell me? You never even mentioned it in your letters. Not a word.

BABA.   I was embarrassed.

NELLY.   Embarrassed? Why?

BABA.   Oh well . . . you know, Nelly. Middle-aged housewife . . . dreams of fame and all that. I even go to an evening class in playwriting. It's all a bit ridiculous, I know that.

NELLY *(leafing through the pages)*.   I can't get over it. Of course you were always **going** to write. For as long as I can remember.

BABA.   Oh absolutely. Then one day I thought — they'll probably put that on my tombstone. 'She was always going to write.' So I started. I mean I know I'll never really be any good at it. I get terribly depressed and sort of infuriated and I keep thinking I'll just give it up but I don't. I'm what you'd call obsessed.

NELLY *(lightly. Slight sting)*.   Lucky you.

BABA *(edgy)*.   You're sending me up.

NELLY *(note of sadness)*. No.

BABA *(after a brief pause . Awkward)*.   Well what do you think, Nelly? The story thus far etcetera.

NELLY.   I think it's terrific.

BABA *(glad)*.   You do?

NELLY.   Yes.

BABA *(depressed)*.   I don't believe you.

NELLY.   Would you believe me if I said it was terrible?

BABA.   Yes.

NELLY.   You know it isn't.

BABA.   I don't, I don't!

NELLY *(slight irritation)*.   Well that's just silly. How many plays have you written anyway?

BABA.   This is the fourth.

NELLY.   So what does your evening-class teacher think of it?

BABA.   God, I don't know. He just goes on and on about structure and character development and things.

NELLY.   Well what did he think of the other three?

BABA *(shudders)*.   He never saw them! Nobody did. I only started going to the class this term. *(Pause)* I say nobody saw them. Several dozen theatres did. And the BBC . . . one of them was a radio play. Nobody wanted them of course. *(Depressed)* Why would they? (NELLY *strikes a pose and sings in the same operatic contralo* BABA *used earlier.)*

NELLY.   Be not downhearted dear friend. Your day will come.

BABA *(delighted)*.   Oh Nelly! You still do the Opera Singer.

NELLY.   All the time. It's my favourite. *(Then through a yawn)* Oh dear. Sorry.

BABA.   You should go back to bed. It's terribly early! You've only had about three hours sleep. Plus your jet lag. And me forcing you to read my play.

NELLY.   You didn't force me . . . I asked.

BABA.   I think I probably organised you into asking. *(Pause. Then not looking at her. Awkward again)* And I feel awful because we haven't talked about Ronnie at **all.**

NELLY *(quickly)*.   I don't want to. I told you.

BABA *(bit helpless)*.   Oh Nelly . . . *(Pause)* I just feel as though I've . . . I mean last night was when you and I should have . . . *(breaks off)* My fault for letting Joe drive me out to the airport. I should have come by myself. And when we all got back here there just didn't seem to be any moment for —

NELLY *(interrupts. Slightly sharp)*.   It doesn't matter! *(Brief pause. Then leafs through pages)* This Eli character sounds a bit like Joe. Did you mean him to?

BABA *(taken aback)*.   No I didn't. Does he? *(Pause)* Yes I suppose he does. That's the trouble with writing a play about marriage. Your own keeps seeping in.

NELLY.   The Annie one is like you. *(Pause. Thoughtful)* And not like you.

BABA.   She's ten years younger than me and a much nicer person. I hope. (NELLY *laughs. A short silence.)*

NELLY.   Do you write every day, Baba?

BABA.   Not weekends. I can only do it when there's nobody in the house. *(Pleasure)* I wait until they go out in the morning. Well . . . they. Joe, now. I usually get started about —

NELLY *(interrupting)*.   What have you done with all the furniture in here by the way?

BABA.   What? Oh, I moved the whole lot up into the attic.

NELLY.   So what does the 'little one' do when she comes home for the hols?

BABA.   The latest bulletin from the 'little one' was that she isn't ever coming home at all.

NELLY.   Oh yes? I did notice she hadn't cropped up much in the conversation. The only thing I've heard about Ginger so far is Joe saying she's in a tutorial college in Banbury. Why Banbury?

BABA *(grim)*.   Just to get away from me. *(Pause)* Not my absolutely favourite topic these days, my daughter. Have a cigarette. Oh God I forgot. This is very hard on me, you giving up. *(Aggrieved)* You taught me how to smoke. How long ago did you stop anyway?

NELLY *(smug)*.   Nine years . . . no, nine and a half.

BABA.   Oh God, Nelly it's really **true** that we haven't seen each other for ten years!

NELLY *(nods)*.   A decade.

BABA.   How awful that is.

NELLY.   Yes. *(There is a pause.)*

BABA *(slightly forced)*.   And we've been smoking together since we were fourteen years old and now you've forsaken me. Some friend. All you care about is your lungs and your heart and your life expectancy.

NELLY.   I've always been selfish. Just can't help it.

BABA.   Very sneaky not to say anything about it in your letters.

NELLY.   Not sneaky — superstitious. I was afraid if I wrote it down . . . especially to you, Baba . . . I'd just start again.

BABA.   A likely story. Don't palter with me, mate.

NELLY.   Palter?

BABA.   It's in Shakespeare somewhere. It means . . . I dunno . . . like double talk. I think.

NELLY.   Oh. Hmmm. Palter . . . I always used to wonder about 'fardels'. 'Who would fardels bear to grunt and sweat under a weary life' and that. *(Laughs)* Fardels! Sounds so rude.

BABA *(laughing too)*.   What's it from anyway?

NELLY *(surprised)*.   Hamlet. Slings and arrows, the proud man's whatsit and all the rest of it. Goodness, imagine you not knowing that! Always head of the class in Eng. Lit. **You** used to read Shakespeare for fun.

BABA.   I didn't really. I just said I did.

NELLY.   I might have known. You were always a cheat and a liar.

BABA.   So were you.

NELLY.   True. *(Through another yawn)* That's probably why we're best friends.

BABA.   Go back to bed, Nelly.

NELLY.   I wouldn't sleep. I've become a semi-professional insomniac since . . . *(Breaks off. Then lightly again)* Do you know something, Baba? *(Taps script)* I really do envy you this play of yours. I don't do anything. *(Pause)* Never have when you come right down to it.

BABA.   Oh come on. You've had two children just for a start.

NELLY.   So? You've had three.

BABA.   Oh honestly, Nelly. You've travelled all over the world and you speak about nine languages —

NELLY *(interrupts)*.   And I embroider beautifully and I'm a first rate hostess and a cracking cook and on **my** tombstone they'll put —she was never going to do anything worth doing because it seemed safer not to. *(Pause. Slight laugh. Surprised at herself)* Sounds awfully bitter.

BABA.   Yes. *(Awkward)* Are you?

NELLY *(brisk)*.   I really don't know. Though I must admit I haven't had many bright ideas about how to spend my 'declining years'. *(Resonant)* Wealthy widow. *(Shrugs)* Doesn't sound like me but that's exactly what I am. *(Pause. Bright)* Perhaps I should buy a racehorse . . . *(bit bleak)* or a yacht or something. *(Another silence.)*

BABA *(bit over-casual)*.   Do you think you'll stay in England now, Nelly?

NELLY *(vivacious)*.   I have no idea. I have absolutely no idea whatever. My mind is a total blank. I don't seem to be able to decide anything at all. *(Pause. Looks at BABA. Smiles)* That's why I've come all this way, Baba. You're to decide the whole thing for me. Plan my future.

BABA *(blankly)*.   What?

NELLY.   Only a joke. Just a joke. *(Pause)* As a matter of fact the boy in your play . . . what's his name? Raymond? Yes . . . Raymond. *(Looks through pages)* Where is it? He says something when he's shouting at his mother through the door.

RAYMOND *comes in. He is about sixteen and dressed in jeans, T shirt and sneakers. NELLY and BABA unaware of him.*

NELLY & RAYMOND *(in unison, RAYMOND shouting, NELLY just reading)*.   There's nobody in here and I'm not talking to anybody.

RAYMOND.   I wish there was! Maybe they'd tell me what I'm supposed to do!

NELLY *(looks up)*.   That's just how I feel. *(Pause. BABA looks at her baffled and upset)*

BABA.   Oh Nelly, listen . . . I —

NELLY *(interrupting)*.   He's very nice, this Raymond. Made me laugh all that stuff he says about people's cover. Oh yes *(leafs through pages again)* and I love the suicide note bit.

RAYMOND, *who has frozen while they are talking, takes a crumpled paper out of his pocket. Reads.*

RAYMOND.   I'm thinking in terms of booking a hotel room in Tangier and taking an overdose. *(Pause. Thoughtful)* Or Felixstowe. *(Reads again)* This suicide note is just to say that I couldn't bear life any longer because I'd discovered *(relish)* that my parents were spying for the Russians! *(Glancing off stage as to ANNIE outside the door. Loud. Spiteful)* Then you'll have to be **investigated** and interrogated and everything and that'll take your mind off your grief!

NELLY *(looks up. Laughs. RAYMOND freezes)*.   He's a monster, Baba! But you can't help liking him.

BABA *(pleased)*.   You're supposed to.

NELLY.   How old is he?

BABA.   Sixteen.

NELLY.   Oh really? Ho ho! But not at a tutorial college in Banbury
. . . eh?

BABA.   All right . . . *(They smile at each other.)*

NELLY.   Tell you something I noticed. Both the men in this play get to
talk to themselves but the woman doesn't. Is that because she's so well
balanced or something?

BABA.   No, it's because I'm always talking to **my**self.

NELLY *(laughs).*   Oh God . . . me too. Well, like this bit at the
beginning. *(Leafs through pages)* Before the piano-tuner arrives. Is Eli
supposed to be talking to himself? Or is he praying or what?

During the above JOE *comes in and* RAYMOND *goes out.* JOE *kneels on
the floor between* BABA *and* NELLY *who are quite unaware of him.*

JOE *(clasps hands).*   Hello out there. *(Looks up)* Hello up there. *Closes
eyes)* Hello in there. *(Pause)* Anybody home? *(Pause)* Probably not.
(He remains kneeling with his eyes closed.)

BABA.   Well sort of praying, yes. Perhaps. Thing is, I just don't know if
you can get away with what you might call the out-and-out soliloquy
anymore. I mean I think it's considered very old fashioned. It seemed
like it might be more . . . you know . . . acceptable to the audience if—
(Breaks off. Gets up. Speaks rather angrily). And that makes me feel like
a total idiot just saying that. Audience. I mean nobody is ever going to
put the bloody thing on so why do I even—

NELLY.   They might.

BABA.   Don't humour me, Nelly.

NELLY.   I'm not.

BABA.   It doesn't happen to people like me.

NELLY *(slightest edge of unpleasantness).*   What's so marvellous about
people like you?

BABA *(completely taken aback).*   You know I didn't mean that. I—

NELLY *(friendly).*   Well shut up, then.

She goes back to the script and reads the following in unison with JOE.

NELLY & JOE.   I'm not asking anybody for anything.

JOE.   Or at least it doesn't seem likely to me that I am. I don't expect it, I
don't deserve it, I wouldn't know what to do with it if they gave it to me.
(Pause) It? *(Pause)* They? *(Pause. Conversational)* For example, how
has it come about that inclination — stroke — passion should have come
to play so small a part in my life? These days. Well no part at all as far as I
can make out. You **could** say, I think, that all my desires are withered and
yet at the same time my withers are unwrung. *(Pause. Idly)* What about
the old hackles? How are they?

During the above NELLY *continues looking at the script.* BABA *is
standing, not watching, but listening.*

NELLY *(looking over at* BABA*).*   Why 'Eli'?

BABA.   I don't know, I just sort of liked the name. Names are hard.

NELLY *nods and looks back down at the script.*

JOE.   Guilt now . . . that's all in order. That still ticks over. Like the heartbeat of some small but particularly repugnant animal that I am obliged to carry around inside me. *(Pause)* Lodged somewhere between the gall bladder and the *(pause)* rectum, perhaps. A two headed animal. Two separate varieties of guilt coinciding. Cohabiting. In me. The cosmic or overall guilt on the one hand e.g. why are other people wiped out by earthquake, famine, bombs, air disasters etcetera whereas I am not and the specific or nub-like guilt which is that I am making the only person I care about in the world unhappy. *(Pause)* Also her son. *(Pause)* Well, my son. *(Pause)* If indeed he is. My son. *(Looks up, clasping hands again. Intense)* Is he my son? *(There is a pause. Then he goes slowly forward into the all-fours position. Staring at the floor)* Hello down there. *(Pause)* Nobody. *(After a moment or two* BABA *walks over to him and sits down on his back. There is a pause.* JOE *doesn't react.)*

BABA *(bright).*   What are you doing? Looking for your contact lenses?

JOE *(calm).*   No. Could you get off my back do you think, Annie?

BABA.   By all means.

She gets up and watches him begin to crawl out of the room. She goes and picks up the radio and turns it on very loud. It's still the second movement of the Dvorak Cello Concerto. JOE *immediately jumps to his feet and almost runs to her, seizes the radio and turns it off.*

JOE.   For Christ's sake, Annie!

He hands the radio back to her in silence. They look at each other and then he turns and goes off. BABA *returns the radio to its original position. Looks over* NELLY'S *shoulder at the script.*

BABA *(thoughtful).*   'Is he my son?' Bit melodramatic.

NELLY.   Oh I don't know. Like what music would be playing on the radio?

BABA.   Probably the Dvorak Cello Concerto. *(She turns the radio on again and the music plays again.)*

NELLY *(startled).*   My God, Baba, how did you do that? Is the radio in your power or what?

BABA *(laughs).*   No, it's a cassette recorder, you fool. I am sort of insane about this concerto at the moment. I play it all the time . . . and cry.

NELLY.   Bit declassé crying over Dvorak wouldn't you say? *(Kindly)* I myself cry over Mozart.

BABA.   Snob.

BABA *turns the music down and it plays quietly during the following section.*

NELLY   *(listens to it).* Well it is nice. It's very nice. *(A pause while they both listen contentedly together. Peaceful)* I'm very glad to be here, Baba.

BABA *(ditto).*   I'm glad too. *(Then a little sad)* Ten years . . .

NELLY.   Mmmm. You know something, Baba?

BABA.   What?

NELLY.   In the last twenty-seven years you and I have only seen each other for a total of fifty-two days.

BABA.   No . . . surely not.

NELLY.   I counted them up. And that always surrounded by husbands and children or in airports.

BABA.   And when you think, Nelly, from when we were what? Twelve to . . . **twenty**, we saw each other every day near enough.

NELLY *(pause to calculate)*.   Nearly three thousand days. *(Again they listen to the music.)*

BABA.   Your fault. Always moving to far off lands.

NELLY.   Not mine . . . Ronnie's. I had to go where they posted him.

BABA.   Nelly . . .

NELLY.   Mmm?

BABA.   I'm sorry that letter I wrote to you about Ronnie was so hopeless. I just didn't know how to say anything about it all.

NELLY *(smiles at her)*.   It's all right.

BABA *(awkward)*.   Do you miss him a lot?

NELLY *(simply)*.   No. *(Pause)* He seemed so old.

BABA *(not looking at her)*.   Well he was. Old enough to be your father. *(Pause.)*

NELLY.   Do you know . . . that repugnant animal that your Eli says he carries around inside him . . . the guilt thing.

BABA.   Yes?

NELLY *(sad)*.   That'll be a fardel I'll bet. (BABA *looks at her*. NELLY *turns off the radio.)* I was glad when he died, Baba. *(Pause)* Are you shocked?

BABA.   No. *(Then looks away)* No . . . it just makes me feel nervous to hear you say it.

NELLY *(sighs)*.   Yes. *(Pause. Then brisk)* Now. Tell me about Ginger.

BABA.   Nelly . . .

NELLY *(interrupting)*.   No really. I want to know.

BABA.   Well . . . *(then brightly)* All right . . . take the last year. Semi-professional truant, juvenile court on a marijuana charge, a phantom pregnancy . . .

NELLY.   What?

BABA.   Mmm hmm. Last summer. We all believed it — even the family doctor. The urine sample she took in for testing was donated by a generous pregnant friend it turned out. I got very frantic and managed to arrange an abortion. Then . . . what do you know! The whole thing a joke. Ha ha.

NELLY.   Jesus Christ!

BABA.   Hasn't lifted a finger as far as I can make out.

NELLY *(laughs)*.   Honestly, Baba! What if the nuns heard you? *(Prim Irish voice)* Oh Barbara, do you think you can hurt heaven with your cheap and childish blasphemy? Don't you know that Our Lord has a sense of humour? He's laughing at you, Barbara.

BABA *(grim)*.   That's certainly the way it feels.

NELLY.   Oh stop . . . *(She laughs again and BABA laughs too.)*

BABA.   I don't know why I'm laughing. It's not a bit funny, really.

NELLY.   Ginger . . . well! Little Virginia . . . sweet sixteen.

BABA.   Sweet.

NELLY.   Well there's no need to make such a big thing about it, Baba, it's normal. Both of mine were calamitous at that age. So were your twins . . . don't you remember? They were driving you and Joe up the wall last time I was here. You've just forgotten all that because Ginger's so much younger than all our other children. How does Joe cope with her?

BABA.   Oh fine. Fine. He thinks she's funny. And he's the one she confides in . . . when she does. Which also depresses me.

NELLY.   I expect she reminds him of you when you two first met.

BABA.   What? I wasn't a bit like Ginger. I was diffident and shy.

NELLY.   Get away. You were well known as one of the most eccentric girls at university.

BABA.   That was just a reaction from the convent.

NELLY *(laughs)*.   Oh don't. Remember those terrible school uniforms? I've still got that picture of our class. We look like parcels abandoned by fleeing refugees.

BABA *(laughs)*.   Well quite. If I was a tiny bit bizarre at university it was only because I was basically so repressed and insecure. Covering up.

NELLY.   Maybe that's what Ginger's doing.

BABA.   Oh no. With Ginger everything is Up Front and Hanging Out. Sometimes I think I'm just jealous of her. Which makes me even more depressed. I can't help it, I am! *(Takes out a cigarette. Looks at NELLY. Puts it back)* And it's making me feel **extremely** insecure that you don't smoke and I do.

NELLY.   Well you're more or less obliged to, Baba. You writers, eh? The black coffee, the brimming ashtray . . .

BABA *(angry)*.   Shut up, Nelly. Don't you start!

NELLY *(taken aback)*.   Sorry, I —

BABA.   Just like Joe. Jocular. Patronising.

NELLY *(distressed)*.   Oh Baba honestly I didn't mean . . . I was only . . . *(then in lisping little kid's voice)* I was only being fatuous and asinine, Uncle Reg. (BABA *stares at her astonished. Then realisation dawns.)*

BABA *(deep, man's voice)*.   You were being damned impertinent, laddy, that's what you were being. One more word out of you and we'll bring back flogging. *(They laugh delightedly)* Uncle Reg . . . my God! *(shakes her head, smiling)* My God. What was your one's name? I can't remember.

NELLY *(reproachful)*.   Oh Baba . . . Dinkum! You can't have forgotten Dinkum. *(Kid's voice again)* I say, Uncle Reg, can I have a fardel? All the chaps at school have fardels, Uncle Reg. *(Own voice)* Anyway he wasn't my one. We were both both, don't you remember?

BABA.   Of course we were. Of course. *(Laughs again. Then in little kid's voice)* Good news, Uncle Reg! I flushed my dad down the loo this morning.

NELLY *(as Uncle Reg)*.   Absolute waste of time that, boy. He'll be back. Piece of cake the whole sewage system to your dad. Eats it up!

BABA *(laughs)*.   Oh stop it. We weren't that disgusting.

NELLY.   We were. It was our way of grappling with puberty.

BABA.   How weird I should forget Uncle Reg and Dinkum. I've always
remembered the Opera Singer.

NELLY *(sings in operatic contralto)*.   The Opera Singer was never
obscene.

BABA *(ditto)*.   Perish the thought. *(They laugh again.)*

NELLY.   Oh dear, how sad it is eh? Two pathetic little girls. All those
potty voices and silly games.

BABA.   Yes. *(Pause)* Although no one could have regarded me as little.
Do you recall how my dad always called me Jumbo?

NELLY *(bit grim)*.   I do recall that, yes. But it doesn't make you any less
pathetic just because you were a bit fat.

BABA.   Obese.

NELLY *(affectionate)*. Oh shut up.

BABA *(after a pause)*.   I suppose we were both just extremely deprived.
Orphans clinging together in the storm. Well, half orphans.

NELLY *(slight unpleasant edge)*.   You were. I didn't achieve half-orphan
status until 1950 . . . don't you remember?

BABA *(hurt)*.   Nelly! Don't. That's not fair.

NELLY.   Sorry. *(Pause)* I'm sorry, Baba. *(Then brightly)* When you think
about it I suppose it's amazing that we're not more twisted than we are.
(Deliberately changing the subject) So what's going to happen next in
your play?

BABA *(depressed immediately)*.   I don't know. Have a grape.

NELLY *(taking one)*.   You must know. You're writing it.

BABA.   I really don't. It's a sort of experiment in not planning ahead.
(Takes several grapes. Then mouth full) A failed experiment. I always
knew this play wasn't going to work.

NELLY.   It does work, Baba. You're silly.

BABA.   Well the teacher at this college keeps telling me I should have got
lots more exposition in by now. He says for the first three scenes you
can't even tell if Annie and Eli are married.

NELLY.   Oh rubbish, of course you can. He sounds a bit of a nerd.

BABA.   He isn't, he's nice. He's only about twenty-five.

NELLY.   Ah ha.

BABA.   Get off. He's got no chin and bifocals, poor little thing. What's
good about him is he does make you work. Five more pages by next
Tuesday sort of thing.

NELLY.   Well you can tell him from me it's perfectly obvious that Eli and
Annie are married. I mean in that first scene where he comes in and says
to her . . .

She is leafing through the pages when the door opens and JOE *comes in. (As*
JOE, *not* ELI)

JOE.   Failure! Total and particular. Global and microscopic. Failure!

BABA *gets up and slips the notebook into the desk drawer very offhandedly
as she moves toward him.*

BABA.   Failure? *(Annoyed)* What do you mean?

JOE. I mean the morning's tasks. My little expedition. Disaster. In every respect. In toto in short.

NELLY *(laughs).* Oh Joe . . . listen to you!

JOE *(kisses her cheek).* Morning Nelly, did you get any sleep at all?

NELLY. Oh about thirty-nine winks.

BABA. What disaster?

JOE. You're right of course. Too strong a word. Let's just say . . . disappointment. Yes, a series of minor but cruel disappointments. The stationers unaccountably closed, the dry cleaning ticket lost, nobody anywhere having ripe avocados in stock, the fishmonger having failed to put by the salmon trout . . . and the car broke down. You see before you Prometheus Bound.

NELLY *(laughs again).* Prometheus Bound . . .

JOE *(beams at her).* Talking too much. It's the excitement of seeing you again.

NELLY. You're just the same. How can anybody go on being so exactly the same?

JOE. What? No no. Au contraire. Absolutely not. *(Indignant)* The same? Balding, look. And a pot belly. Ask Baba . . . she never stops nagging about it. I quite like it myself. I fold my hands across it. *(Demonstrates)* Nice don't you think? Oh yes, ageing away here, slouching towards Bethlehem, out out brief candle . . . all that sort of thing.

BABA. Lost the dry cleaning ticket how? Where?

JOE. That's another funny thing. Hadn't lost it at all. Found it on the back seat when the car broke down. Which added a certain je ne sais quoi to the whole experience. (NELLY *laughs some more.)*

BABA. You only encourage him. He'll just go on and on.

JOE. Sorry about the no avocados and the no salmon trout, Mrs Woman. *(He goes to* BABA, *takes her hands and kisses them.)* And the car. Though it did occur to me we could all go out to lunch in a taxi.

BABA *(surprised).* Mrs Woman?

JOE. The fishmonger said that to the person in front of me. Sorry Mrs Woman. Didn't say sorry Mr Man to me about the salmon trout.

NELLY. Probably thought you'd think he was making gay advances. *(Waves at* JOE) Hi there, Mr Man! *(She and* JOE *laugh.* BABA *is still irritable.)*

BABA. I don't mind about the salmon and the avocados . . . I'd much rather go out to lunch than cook . . . but I did want that dress for tonight.

JOE. Ah, now here is one of life's little problems that Mr Man can solve. *(Holds up cleaning ticket)* We can stop by for the dress in the taxi.

BABA. Oh. All right. Yes.

NELLY. Joe, I never asked you last night . . . how's the new job going?

JOE. New? Four years.

NELLY. No! Well . . . last time I was here you were still in the City. Always seemed so posh, that. Merchant Banker.

JOE. Only a high class usurer, really. Neither a borrower nor a lender be and there I was both.

BABA.   He suddenly realised he'd have been one of the ones Jesus threw out of the temple.

JOE *(looks at her for a moment)*. Do you know you almost invariably say that when the subject of my job change comes up.

BABA.   I don't do I?

JOE.   Yes. *(To* NELLY*)* Baba likes to make it all sound like some kind of profound spiritual conversion. Which it wasn't.

BABA.   Well you were terribly depressed.

JOE *(edge)*.   Not depressed, bored.

NELLY *(slight embarrassment)*.   Well it's still . . . I mean it's a fantastic thing to do. Giving up a smart job and going to work for a charity.

JOE.   Doesn't feel all that fantastic. Fund-raiser, money-maker . . . I do exactly the same things only for different people.

NELLY.   Well but isn't that the point?

JOE.   I suppose so. Yes I should think so. *(Pause)* I expect if you went and handed out actual food to actual people you might feel more . . . *(breaks off)* But then no doubt the old drop in the ocean thing would get you down. Not to mention the fact that the people you were handing out to had got where they were partly thanks to merchant bankers the world over. And then you might start wondering if there was a point at all.

BABA.   Now you are being depressing.

JOE.   So I am. *(light)* You must be half mad with exhaustion both of you Mrs Women. Bed at three this morning and up again at the crack? Madcaps. There was I doing the early morning tea round. No takers. Empty beds everywhere stretching to infinity. Murmur of girlish prattle from behind closed doors. Didn't like to intrude.

NELLY.   You wouldn't have intruded. Baba was just showing me her play.

JOE *(astonished)*.   Play? *(There is a silence.)*

BABA *(unconvincingly casual)*.   What about the car anyway? What's wrong with it?

JOE *(after a pause)*. Nothing about the car. There is bugger all wrong with it. I abandoned it in a gutter somewhere. It just doesn't like me driving it. *(Pleasant)* That car despises me. *(He strolls over to the writing-table and sits on it)* Funny thing, Nelly. She told me she was writing a textbook.

BABA.   Joe . . .

JOE *(to* NELLY *still)*.   On table manners in Tierra del Fuego.

NELLY *(looking from one to the other)*.   What?

BABA *snatches the cigarettes, matches and ashtray from the desk and walks away lighting a cigarette.*

BABA.   Funeral customs and ritual in Bali.

JOE.   Oh of course. How silly of me.

NELLY *(confused)*.   A textbook?

BABA.   Not writing it . . . just helping with the research.

JOE.   That's right, and she's been doing an evening-class in anthropology! Working for an Open University degree. *(Smiles at* BABA*)* Haven't you?

BABA *(stubs out cigarette)*.   Joe!

JOE.   Or trying. Hasn't got it yet. Not altogether surprising now I come to
think of it.
BABA *(angry)*. Please!
NELLY *(floundering)*.   I think anthropology's fascinating. I've always —
JOE *(interrupting. Very amiable)*.   Naturally we all knew this Open
University thing was a lie. Of course. We weren't born yesterday. I
knew, Ginger knew, Baba's dad knew . . . I expect the cat knew. We
didn't talk about it. Just smiled at each other from time to time. There
she goes, we thought, finding herself. Funny little thing.
NELLY *(upset)*.   Joe . . .
JOE.   I had always thought novel, you see. Thinly disguised
autobiographical and tremendously long, of course. Play . . . Well, well.
Play never occurred to me. *(Polite to* BABA*)* Or plays perhaps? I can see
that plays could be ever so much more therapeutic than novels. Up there
in the middle of the stage . . . hello world! Listen to **me.** Gosh yes.
BABA *(very upset)*.   Why are you being so horrible?
JOE.   Because I don't like secrets.
BABA.   It isn't a secret. It's just something private.
JOE.   Well why lie about it? Why all those elaborate lies for Christ's sake?
It's ludicrous. Did you really think I believed all that?
BABA.   Yes I did.
JOE.   My God. I'm a booby then . . . right? Is that what I am?
BABA.   I just wanted to be left alone. I didn't want you making jokes
about it.
JOE.   I wouldn't.
BABA.   Oh yes you would. You never stopped making jokes about the
textbook.
JOE.   Because I knew it was a **lie** and I naturally took it for granted that
you knew I knew. My God, Baba —
BABA.   I know **you.** Just like my father always was. If I got serious about
anything then it had to be funny. Barbara and her laughable little hobby.
Women are supposed to be serious about the housekeeping and the
cooking and scrubbing out the toilet!
JOE.   Wait a minute, what is this? Not only a booby but a chauvinist pig
now. I am neither! And I am not like your bloody father. Am I, Nelly?
NELLY.   No you aren't, and speaking of Baba's father —
BABA *(interrupting)*.   They're all alike that way, men. Even though a lot
of them pretend not to be. Basically they don't approve of women doing
things of their own. Separate things that aren't in any way connected to
hearth or home or coffee mornings.
JOE.   Bloody ridiculous!
BABA.   Yes it is ridiculous and it's true! Nelly . . . you told me it used to
make Ronnie nervous if he ever saw you reading non-fiction.
NELLY.   Well biography was okay. But Ronnie was different, Baba.
BABA.   No he wasn't. They're all like Ronnie except he didn't mind
showing it. The root of the whole thing is that they're envious of women
being able to make babies.
JOE.   Oh really! Anyway . . . not without men they can't.

BABA.   I mean grow them. Creation. Men are afraid of women having that kind of power.

JOE *(laughs)*.   For God's sake, Baba, what have you been reading?

BABA *(furious)*.   Oh of course! It couldn't be anything I thought of myself. It has to be out of a book. Or a feminist tract and therefore comic. Naturally!

NELLY.   Well it did sound a bit like something you might read on a tee-shirt, Baba.

JOE.   You see? Nelly's on my side.

NELLY *(snaps)*.   No I'm not. You two have always done this. Trying to get me on your side against the other.

JOE.   All right. Well at least tell her she's talking codswallop.

NELLY.   Why should I? Maybe it isn't. For example . . . during the course of my rather tedious travels around the globe from army post to army post I met an awful lot of men who clearly felt what I think would have to be called threatened by accomplished women. So consequently there were a lot of **women** I knew who did nothing all the time in order to keep them calm.

BABA.   Exactly!

JOE.   I've obviously stumbled on a tiny consciousness raising group here. *(Backing out)* Pardon me, ladies . . . oh sorry that's sexist isn't it. Pardon me, **women.**

BABA.   Here we go. Reach for the condescending quip, chaps, we might be losing a bit of ground.

JOE.   All right, all right, let's just leave it shall we. You're not writing novels or plays or sonnets or limericks or anything that might frighten me. You're researching a textbook because that's something I can tell the boys in the changing-room without frightening them. And as for all your accomplished non-achieving friends, Nelly, consider the possibility that they may do nothing because that's the way they want it. They can blame all their intellectual and creative frustration on their nervous husbands and go **on** doing nothing. What women are **really** good at is manouvering themselves into the victim position and then complaining about it. That Strindberg knew a thing or two. And . . . *(He goes to* BABA *and takes the cigarettes from her)* It's time you gave up smoking. *(And goes out.* BABA *folds her arms tightly and stands in silence.)*

NELLY *(after a pause)*.   You all right?

BABA *(goes and sits down)*.   Yes. *(Then with intensity)* Sometimes I really hate him!

NELLY.   Why didn't you tell me he didn't know about you and your plays?

BABA.   I don't know.

NELLY.   Perhaps you wanted him to find out.

BABA.   Why?

NELLY.   I don't know. *(Pause)* I'd forgotten he could be such a bastard. What I was trying to say about Ronnie was—

BABA *(interrupting)*.   The thing Joe can't bear is losing an argument. He has to win.

NELLY. Yes but in one way it's a **good** thing that you and Joe —

BABA *(interrupting)*. Good! *(Points at where* JOE *has gone out)* That's what he always does. I hate it! He gets the last word every time . . . and then goes out before you can answer back. If that's what you think is **good** you can have it.

NELLY. That's just the point, Baba. Ronnie and I never —

BABA *(interrupting again)*. God, he can be so bossy and boring. I'd really like to leave him sometimes you know, Nelly.

NELLY *(simply telling her)*. No you wouldn't.

BABA. I don't know. Sometimes I don't even know if we really love each other anymore. We're attached. That's the problem. We're not two separate people . . . we're a couple. I think what marriage is all about is chopping bits of yourself off that don't fit with the other person and growing bits that do. Your other half. *(Sighs)* How depressing that is.

NELLY *(factual)*. Pretending's worse.

BABA *(not listening)*. Mmmm. And the thing is if you actually left your other half you'd be sort of deformed I suppose. All those bits broken off.

NELLY *(looks at her for a moment and then turns away)*. Well that was no doubt Mother Nature's plan.

BABA *(sulky)*. What a shit he is.

NELLY (turning back. Tart). No he isn't. And you do love him and so do I.

BABA. Yes. I wish you didn't.

NELLY. You're being silly.

BABA *(childish)*. I am not.

Again NELLY *regards her. Then she strikes an Uncle Reg attitude.*

NELLY *(very genial. Uncle Reg voice)*. Ah laddie, laddie cast your mind back. College days . . . eh? All freshmen together in the frolicsome fifties, what? Sprintin' about in Regents Park, a touch of your Dvoraks in the Albert Hall, Lyons Corner House, all those —

BABA *(interrupts in malevolent Dinkum voice)*. Shove it up your ass, Uncle Reg!

NELLY *(laughs)*. Oh Baba . . .

BABA *(mild)*. Wish I had a cigarette.

NELLY. Oh listen I got you some at the Duty Free. I'll get them. *(Starts out. Stops)* Baba . . . your father. He is still in Canada isn't he.

BABA. Nope. Came back. Six months ago.

NELLY. My God how terrible. Why?

BABA. Suddenly seized by the desire to spend the autumn of his life near his little girl. The moment he saw me when we met him at the airport he screamed and hid under a chair.

NELLY *(laughs. Amazed)*. What?

BABA. He did. And he wouldn't let anybody but Joe touch him.

NELLY. But he always hated Joe!

BABA. Not now. He loves Joe. He loves everybody . . . except me. He's become a sort of saint person.

NELLY. Your **father?**

BABA. It's all an act of course — although nobody seems to know that
except me. He's in an extremely expensive Old People's Home near
Guildford. Spends all his time being sweet and pious and whimsical.
They all adore him . . . and he's got them eating out of his hand.

NELLY. The old devil!

BABA. No no! That's what he tells everybody I am. In the middle of all
this mad frenzy out at the airport he started accusing me of being an
imposter. Shouting to everybody . . . and I mean everybody . . . that I
wasn't his daughter at all but a doppelganger and that I wanted to kill
him. *(Pause)* Which I did. I had to come back on the bus! I'm not allowed
to visit him at the home. Matron says I upset him. I upset him!
Everybody out there thinks I am Goneril and Regan and Snow White's
stepmother rolled into one. And whenever he comes here I have to go
out before he arrives and not come back till he goes.

NELLY *(laughs).* Oh my God, Baba. I should have been with you for all
that.

BABA. You couldn't have been. Ronnie wasn't dead yet.

NELLY stares at her and then begins helplessly to laugh.

NELLY. Baba!

BABA *(appalled realisation).* Oh Nelly . . . I wasn't thinking. Oh how
could I? I just —

NELLY *(overcome with laughter).* Don't . . . don't . . .

*And BABA begins to laugh too. For a moment or two they are both
convulsed. Gradually they stop, subsiding into exhausted silence.*

BABA *(blows her nose).* What a fool I am.

NELLY *(moving towards her. Purposeful).* Baba, listen . . .

BABA *(not listening).* **And** I feel such a fool Joe finding out about the
play. And I don't even know why. Why didn't I want him to know?
(NELLY *looks at her in silence for a moment.)*

NELLY *(businesslike).* Well I'll go and get you those fags.

BABA *(grateful).* Thanks, Nelly.

*NELLY goes and BABA stretches and yawns. She takes the notebook out of
the drawer of the table and idly leafs through the pages. Stops at one page and
reads to herself. RAYMOND comes on from the side.*

BABA & RAYMOND *(in unison).* He enjoyed talking to me.

RAYMOND. I asked him if I could come and live with him. *(With relish)*
I begged him to take me away from here. (BABA *turns and makes a
move away from the table.)*

BABA. The piano tuner?

RAYMOND. Yes. He was a very nice man. I liked him.

BABA. Raymond. He must have thought you were mad.

RAYMOND. I am.

BABA. Don't start that again.

RAYMOND. I told him I was retarded. *(Angry emphasis)* Which I am!

BABA.   Oh sweetheart . . .

RAYMOND *(mocking)*.   Oh mummy . . . *(then reasonable)* I am emotionally stunted because my father despises me.

BABA *(amused)*.   Melodrama.

RAYMOND.   All right. Because my father doesn't like me. How's that? *(Pause)* Mother? *(Pause)* Well . . . does he?

BABA.   He doesn't like anybody at the moment. He's depressed. He doesn't like me. He doesn't like himself.

RAYMOND.   So I'd rather live with the piano tuner. Mr Albarian. I've packed that blue canvas bag. I told him I'd be arriving about eight.

BABA.   Raymond stop it. It's boring.

RAYMOND.   He's Armenian. Did you know that all Armenian surnames end in i—a—n? I also told him I was a genius. I told him I had an I.Q. of 179 but he wasn't impressed. He was when I played for him, though.

BABA.   I heard you.

RAYMOND.   I hoped you would. Do you know what it was?

BABA.   Beethoven?

RAYMOND.   Very good. Yes. The Farewell Sonata. Farewell Mother.

BABA.   Baby, please stop. This is just what Eli hates so much when you start doing this. It drives him mad.

RAYMOND.   No no, it is he who has driven me mad. *(Sharp)* And how can you be so sure that that isn't true, eh? Eh? You're the only one I don't do it to.

BABA.   You're doing it to me now. 'Farewell Mother.'

RAYMOND.   All right, all right. What I'm saying . . . if you'll listen . . . is that you are the only person I am myself with. My real self. Or could it be that I just trot this one out to please you? The other one might be the real one. The one everybody else sees. *(Pause)* And hates.

BABA.   Don't be silly.

RAYMOND.   I don't mind if they hate me. It's easier.

BABA.   Easier?

RAYMOND *(pleasant)*.   Not to have to try to be likeable. you don't have to worry about being boring and tiresome and generally detestable if people already think you are. You can behave badly the whole time with impunity if you follow me. *(Pause)* Nobody can judge you. The real you I mean. You're safe. *(Light)* You're just an object of contempt.

BABA *(distressed)*.   But why should you want to be?

RAYMOND *(angry)*.   I don't want to be . . . I am! To myself. I know what a stupid useless person I am! I know nobody could ever like me! *(Pause. Light again)* I don't care what they think of the one I'm pretending to be. *(Pause)* It's quite funny.

BABA.   Oh Raymond . . .

RAYMOND.   I can do without them. I don't need any outside help, believe me. I've got enough voices of my own. Inside. Laughing at me all the time. At the things I say, the way I look. What? Self mockery? Self contempt? I'm very good at all that. And of course I have a preternatural gift for paranoia . . .

NELLY *(offstage)*. Baba? (RAYMOND *goes off stage at once. NELLY comes in.)* This is a peace mission. *(Turns back. Calls)* Joe? (JOE *comes in with a tray of glasses and a decanter. BABA hastily returns the notebook back to the drawer.)* I caught him just as he was going out the front door.

BABA *(slightly forced jolly)*. Leaving home, were you?

JOE. No I was just going out to find the car and kick it. *(He puts the tray down and not looking at BABA pours the sherry.)* Sorry about being so disagreeable, Baba. *(He takes BABA her glass.)*

BABA. Joe, you know I wasn't trying to—

JOE *(interrupts. Breezy)*. No post mortem . . . please. All right? *(To NELLY)* Every time Baba and I have a row she wants a kind of analytic seminar about it afterwards. And the worst of it is she's got a photographic memory for the spoken word. What did you mean when you said that . . . what I meant when I said this. All the psychological connections, the historical resonances.

NELLY *(slightly uncomfortable)*. Well but . . . don't you think it could be a good thing to try and find out what it was all about?

JOE. No. *(He has given her her glass. Raises his own.)* Cheers.

NELLY. Cheers.

BABA *(after a brief pause)*. Cheers.

JOE. Damn the torpedos, full speed ahead, eh Baba? (NELLY *laughs. BABA doesn't. She sips her sherry. There is a somewhat awkward silence. Then bright)* Who remembers tprootz?

NELLY. Tprootz?

BABA. What?

JOE. That film that was on when we were at University. Taproots. All those posters round London just saying Taproots in big red letters. So Eric and I . . . you remember Eric.

NELLY. Eric? Oh yes . . . Eric! The one with the teeth. What ever happened to him?

JOE. Who knows? He's probably saying that to people about us at this very moment. Who knows what happened to any of us? Anyway Eric and I decided it wasn't Taproots but tprootz and tprootz were actually **tiny** naked ladies that you could carry around inside your jacket and murmur to and fondle. *(Demonstrates)* And one day we met in the student union bar or somewhere and Eric said let's show each other our tprootz. So I took mine out . . . all fond and proud . . . and I put her on the floor. *(Demonstrates. Stands there looking down and smiling)* And Eric *(demonstrates)* stamped on her!

NELLY. Oh! *(then she laughs)*

BABA *(laughs)*. My God! It's the archetypal sexist myth.

JOE *(pleased)*. Isn't it?

They smile at each other. NELLY puts her glass down on the tray.

NELLY. Well if it doesn't seem rude I think I will go and have a little kip before we go out to lunch.

BABA. Do, Nelly.

NELLY. What time will we leave?

JOE.   Half past one-ish. Catch the pub.

NELLY.   Will someone call me?

BABA.   I will. Would you like a hot bath first?

NELLY.   No thanks. Maybe tonight before the party. *(Starts out. Turns)*
Speaking of which there really is no need to take me along, you know. I
can always go to bed with Agatha Christie as it were.

BABA.   Of course you're coming.

JOE.   Sandy's very keen to meet you, Nelly.

BABA.   And if you don't go, I won't. Vernal Equinox Party! It's so camp.
I don't even know what a vernal equinox is.

NELLY.   It's when the sun crosses the celestial equator.

BABA.   Is it? Anyway the food will be good.

JOE.   And there will be a great deal to drink.

NELLY.   Oh good. *(Pause)* Perhaps we could all get drunk and behave
awfully badly.

JOE.   We can certainly give it a go.

NELLY.   Right! *(She goes. BABA and JOE finish their sherry in silence.)*

JOE.   Oh. *(Takes cigarettes from his pocket. Gives them to her)*

BABA.   Thank you.

JOE *(keeping hold of her hand).*   Baba, there's just one thing I'd like to
say.

BABA *(stares at him disbelievingly).*   What do you **mean?**

There is the sound of a scuffle and voices offstage.

NELLY *(off).*   Who the hell are you?

GINGER *(off).*   Same to you, Lady.

BABA *(horrified).*   Ginger!

GINGER *(off).*   Would you mind letting me pass?

GINGER *comes in followed by NELLY. She's 16 and dressed in elegant
three-piece man's suit. Very pretty. Rather elaborate make-up.*

BABA.   What are you doing here?

GINGER.   Just visiting the old folks at home. Do you mind? Hello Joe,
what do you know?

JOE *(beams at her).*   Hello Ginger. Not a lot. What are you supposed to
look like?

GINGER.   A transvestite. It's to frighten the natives in Banbury. It does
too. *(To NELLY)* Oh I know! You must be Auntie Eleanor, Mummy's
best friend, aren't you.

NELLY.   Well I—

GINGER *(looking around. Angry to BABA).*   What have you done with
all my stuff? This is my room you know. Where's my bed for Christ's
sake? What is this anyway? I'm some kind of typographical error you're
trying to rub out of your life or something?

BABA *(exasperated).*   Oh Ginger . . .

GINGER *(to NELLY).*   Do you know something funny Auntie
Eleanor . . . you don't mind if I call you Auntie Eleanor do you?

NELLY.   As a matter of fact I—

GINGER *(ignoring her)*.   My mother never just says my name. Ginger.
   She simply can't manage it. Ginger. Not too hard is it? With her it's
   either **Gin**ger or Gin**ger**! No wonder I'm so warped. *(To* BABA.
   Affectionate) Guess what? I've got a surprise for you. I left it in the hall.
   Wait till you see it. You'll love it!
BABA.   What is it . . . a boa constrictor?
GINGER *(laughs)*.   See? You can be very witty. You shouldn't get so
   depressed about yourself. Can I have a fag? *(She snatches the pack of
   cigarettes and matches.* BABA *starts to speak.)* **Gin**ger! Gin**ger**! *(Lights
   cigarette. Then in baby voice)* I smoke because I want to be like my
   mummy. *(She chucks the cigarettes and matches onto the floor and starts
   out.)* I'm going to get your surprise now. Back in a flash! *(She goes.*
   BABA *picks up the cigarettes.)*
NELLY.   Dear heaven, I don't remember her like that when she was six.
JOE.   We call it adolescence.
BABA.   We call it purgatory . . . *(horrified)* Oh my God!

*She moves swiftly into the furthest position away from the door and turns her
back. Through the door comes* STANLEY, *her father, 75.* GINGER *is
gently pushing him in from behind.* NELLY *is staring at* BABA.

NELLY.   Baba . . . what are . . . *(turns and sees* STANLEY) Oh!
JOE.   Ginger, you are a thousand kinds of a fool. *(He goes to* STANLEY
   in an attempt to mask BABA.) Hello Stanley, how are you?
STANLEY *(shaking his hand warmly)*.   I don't know your name but I
   know your face. It's a good face . . . an honest face . . . a clean face!
   You could eat your dinner off this face. *(To* NELLY) And who's this?
NELLY.   Hello. I don't know if you—
STANLEY *(stares at her. Suddenly very sharp)*.   Who are you?
NELLY.   I . . .

Instantly benign again, he takes her hand. Heavy West Country accent.

STANLEY.   You'm got lovely eyes, Missy . . . you'm got lovely eyes.
   (Own accent) Born in Shropshire you know. *(Country accent again)* In
   summertime on Bredon, the bells they ring so clear. *(Own accent)* A. E.
   Housman . . . little A. E. Old friend of mine you know. I taught him
   everything he knew about rhyme and metre. (GINGER, *looking at*
   BABA, *tugs at* STANLEY'S *coat.)*
GINGER.   Grandpa . . .
JOE.   Ginger, for God's sake.
NELLY *(intervening)*.   You don't remember me, Mr Phillips. I'm—
STANLEY *(interrupting. Jovial)*.   You mustn't call me Mr Phillips, my
   dear young lady. For one thing it isn't my name. I'm Doctor Renfrew. I
   expect you've heard of me. Consultant psychiatrist at an Old People's
   Home near Guildford. Oh yes, I take care of the poor things. Know my
   secret? Make 'em laugh . . . best medicine in the world. You must call
   me Stanley. Or you could call me Theodore. I always liked the name
   Theo. There's something very — *(breaks off sighting* BABA. *Screams)*
   There she is! She's here!
BABA.   Dad . . .

STANLEY *takes a large cross out of his inside pocket and extends it toward her.*

STANLEY. Don't come near me, devil. I'm in the protection of Our Lady and all the saints. *(Hysterical)* Don't let her touch me. She's Satan's daughter! She'll destroy me! Get her out get her out get her out!
BABA *(furious)*. I'm going.!

As she goes STANLEY *whimpers and dodges away from her waving his cross.*

NELLY. Baba . . . wait. *(Follows BABA off)*
JOE *(going after them)*. Happy, Ginger?
GINGER *(calls after him)*. Yes thanks! *(Laughs)* Oh Grandpa you're fantastic. Satan's daughter! What does that make you, eh?

STANLEY *sinks trembling into the chair kissing the cross and panting.*

STANLEY. Thank you, Lord, oh thank you for saving me from the powers of darkness. *(Then very bright)* Sherry! How nice! *(Pours himself a glass)* And grapes! Well that is kind!

He starts eating the grapes. GINGER *comes over and takes one. He slaps her hand almost absentmindedly and drinks some of his sherry.* GINGER *notices the notbook in the drawer, which is slightly open. She takes it out and, sitting on the edge of the writing-table, she starts to read. The lights dim down to the first circle of light we saw at the beginning of the play and then to black.*

ACT TWO

In the darkness the third movement of the Dvorak Cello Concerto playing quite loud. Lights up on the room. The table is now bare. The stool and the chair are still in the room as well as a very brightly painted toybox (big enough to sit on). Music begins gradually to fade as GINGER *comes through the door dragging a single mattress which she dumps on the floor. She looks round the room with some satisfaction as the music fades to out. She sees the radio/recorder and presses a button. The third movement of the Cello Concerto exactly where it faded out. She listens critically for a moment.*

GINGER. Yuk! *(Turns it off. She opens the toybox and takes out five very battered old cuddly toys and dumps them on the mattress. Arranging the toys, shouts.)* Come on Grandpa! (STANLEY *appears at the door holding Baba's notebook, open.)* You're supposed to be reading to me.
STANLEY. Sorry, cherub. *(Reads)* The room is empty. Suddenly— *(breaks off seeing the mattress. Upset)* Oh. It's not my bedtime is it?
GINGER. No it isn't. Go on. Don't stop.

STANLEY *(reads)*.   Suddenly Raymond runs into the room. He looks
around wildly and then hides under the table.

RAYMOND *runs in and does this. At the same time* GINGER *goes out
through the door again.*

GINGER *(offstage)*.   Louder, Grandpa! I can't hear.
STANLEY *(louder)*.   Hides under the table. There is a pause. then Eli
comes on. He looks round the room not seeing Raymond. *(JOE comes
on and does this. To Himself)* Eli?
JOE.   Raymond?
GINGER.   Grandpa? *(*GINGER *comes on again and* JOE *and
RAYMOND *freeze. She is carrying a deck chair and a bottle of Calvados.
In her pockets she has two glasses.)* Why have you stopped again?
STANLEY *(piteous)*.   I'm an old man, child. These eyes are failing and
these poor bones are crying out to Jesus.
GINGER.   Piss off, Grandpa. You're only seventy-five and you've got
fantastic eyesight and how can a bone cry out? Here. I've brought you
your favourite chair.
STANLEY.   Thank you, lambkin. *(Pats the chair)* Hello old fellow. *(Sits.
Beams at* GINGER*)* Oh what a lovely day I've had!
GINGER *(very pleased)*.   Yeah?
STANLEY.   Oh my goodness. The zoo and all the bus rides and supper in
the West End. Oh ho ho . . . wait till I tell them out at the home. They'll
shrivel up with envy like dead cockroaches!
GINGER *(laughs. Then businesslike)*.   Now listen, Grandpa. Tell me
again what you're going to do when we hear them come back in the taxi.
STANLEY *(concentration)*.   Straight upstairs to bed in the spare room
and don't make a sound. *(Hopeful)* Was that it?
GINGER.   Right! *(Kisses him on the head)* Now. Would you like some
. . . *(reads lable on bottle)* Calvados?
STANLEY *(peevish)*.   No I wouldn't. I don't have to. I won't, I won't, I
won't! I don't need it. I did number twos today. *(More excitable)* I told
Doctor Renfrew I did and if he says I'm a liar then he's a liar! Stupid
spotty common little man! He's nothing but a jumped up—
GINGER.   Grandpa, stop! It isn't a laxative, it's a drink. Like apple juice.
STANLEY.   Oh is it? Then I'll have some.
GINGER *(filling his glass)*.   God you're such a cheater. You only do those
temper tantrums because you enjoy it. None of it's real, is it?
STANLEY *(affable)*.   No no, all in fun.

GINGER *pours her own glass and takes a swig. Gasps, pounds her chest,
eyes watering.*

GINGER.   Jesus!
STANLEY *(smelling his drink)*.   I can't do anything like that out there,
you see. Matron wouldn't like it. Apple juice, eh? *(Drinks off the whole
glassful. No reaction at all)* Though I do sometimes go in for
hallucinations. They're very jolly. *(Rising to his feet, pointing. Terror)*
Matron, save me! There's a goat on the landing with fire coming out of its
mouth. Oh look everybody! It's got a white monkey on its back singing

the Dies Irae! Can't you hear it? It's horrible! *(Sitting again)* That gets them moving around, I'll tell you. Screaming, shouting, trying to get out of the house, knocking each other down, trampling on each other . . . *(smiles reminiscently)* Grand stuff.

GINGER *(laughing).* Go on reading, Grandpa. *(Goes to door. Listens)* They'll be back from that party any minute. I want to hear some more of it.

STANLEY. Does Matron know where I am?

GINGER. Yes, I phoned her. *(Goes to sit on mattress with toys)* I told her you're spending the night here. Oh and I told her Mum was away for the weekend.

STANLEY *(bewildered).* Who? Who was away?

GINGER. Never mind. Go on.

STANLEY *(finding his place).* Raymond puts his hands over his face and huddles further under the table. Eli catches sight of him, bends down to look at him and then stands up with his back to the table. *(As STANLEY reads this JOE and RAYMOND perform it.)*

STANLEY & JOE *(in unison).* I would like the keys to the car. *(There is a pause)*

JOE. I have no desire to embarrass you, Raymond. I know how near the surface your sensibilities lie. Just come out from wherever you are, give me the keys and we can then work our way toward some kind of marginally human conversation. *(After a brief pause RAYMOND throws the keys out from under the table. JOE picks them up.)* Coming out now? *(No answer. Patient)* I said are you coming out. *(No answer)* Right. We'll do it your way. *(He sits cross-legged on the floor facing RAYMOND. As STANLEY speaks they freeze.)*

STANLEY. The snag is you always have to apologise to Matron afterwards. Repent. Hoping she hasn't called snidey little Renfrew in. Who would give his right arm to get the electrodes stuck on to me. *(West Country accent)* Forgive us Matron, we'm know not what we'm do. I'm that sorry for all the upset and for Miss Crary's broken ribs but I just can't help myself. I get the visions awammering and awivering at me and I—

GINGER *(laughing).* Will you leave off. I want more of that play. Here. I'll read it. *(She takes the notebook away from him.)*

STANLEY *(frail).* Oh this is such a treat for me. I do so love to be read aloud to. I know I'm only a bothersome old—

GINGER *(laughs again).* Shut up. *(Reads)* Raymond curls himself up even tighter under the table. His voice is muffled as he shouts furiously at Eli.

RAYMOND. Leave me alone, leave me alone, leave me alone!

JOE. Nothing would give me greater pleasure but before I do I must remind you that, A, you have broken your promise to me and, B—

RAYMOND. I don't know what you mean.

JOE. Yes you do. Six months ago you promised me that you would never steal my car again.

RAYMOND *(very childish).* I didn't steal it, I borrowed it. I wanted to drive Mr Albarian to the station. It's only a mile.

JOE.   It would be the same if it were a hundred yards. You are a totally
   incompetent driver and you don't have a licence. Which brings us, once
   again, to point B . . . the deal that we made. You, having broken your
   promise to me about the car, I will now go forward with the
   arrangements for you to become a boarder at your school.

RAYMOND.   I won't!

JOE *(calm)*.   You will.

There is a pause. RAYMOND *comes out from under the table on his hands
and knees and crawls past* ELI.

RAYMOND *(looking down at the floor)*.   Hello down there. (ELI *leaps to
   his feet and stares at him.*) Hello. Hello. Anybody there. Oh please say
   hello back to me somebody. I've got a two-headed animal stuck up my
   bum. *(Whines)* Get off my back, Annie.

JOE.   You sneaky little eavesdropper!

RAYMOND *(jumping up to face him)*.   I don't have to do anything you
   tell me to do because you aren't my father. I heard you! If he is my son.
   If. *(Melodramatic)* Is he my son? *(Pause)* Well I'm not. I've always—

STANLEY *(yawns rather extensively)*.   I wonder if I could have another
   drop of that apple juice, my treasure. (RAYMOND *and* JOE *freeze*).

GINGER.   Yes okay. *(She gets up, holding the place in the notebook, and
   pours him a glass. Startled)* Listen! Is that the taxi? *(She dumps the
   notebook on his lap and runs out.)*

STANLEY *(imperturbable. Drinks)*.   Delish. *(Surreptitiously, looking at
   the door. He pours himself some more and in doing so drops the
   notebook.)* Oops. *(He picks it up hastily as* GINGER *comes back in.)*

GINGER.   Nope. It's okay.

STANLEY *(ingratiating)*.   Shall I read now, my poppet?

GINGER.   Yeah do. *(She settles herself back on the mattress with her
toys.)*

STANLEY & RAYMOND *(in unison)*.   And of course I have a
   preternatural gift for paranoia.

JOE *goes out immediately and* BABA *comes in wearing the dressing-gown
of Act One.* RAYMOND *sits on the writing-table.*

BABA.   Preternatural . . . paranoia. Well, it alliterates.

She sits in the chair. GINGER *starts to get up, protesting.*

GINGER.   Wait a minute. That's the wrong place.

STANLEY *(calm. Efficient)*.   No no. No no no.

GINGER.   But . . .

STANLEY.´   Shhhh!

STANLEY & BABA *(in unison)*.   Well, it alliterates.

RAYMOND.   If he'd said that I would have wanted to smash his face in.

BABA.   Well, he's your father.

RAYMOND.   Or not.

BABA.   I'm not talking about biology. Whether or not you sprang from
   his actual loins he is your father. The father person in your life since you
   were five weeks old. Whereas I have to share the parental honours with
   an incubator.

RAYMOND. And a corpse. (GINGER, *interested now, sits back listening.*)

BABA *(starts to go)*. Oh well if it's going to be one of those conversations.

RAYMOND. Don't go. I'm sorry.

BABA. Showing off again.

RAYMOND. I can't help it if I've got a mordant wit.

BABA. You just enjoy shocking people.

RAYMOND. I don't particularly enjoy it. It's really just a habit.

BABA. That's worse. *(There is a pause.)*

RAYMOND *(hesitant)*. Mother?

BABA. Yes?

RAYMOND *(passion)*. It wasn't my fault! I didn't kill her!

BABA *(distressed)*. Of course you didn't. Of course not. The car crash killed her. It's a miracle it didn't kill you.

STANLEY *(looks up)*. Wrong. Quite wrong. She didn't die in a car crash. (BABA *and* RAYMOND *freeze*.)

GINGER. What?

STANLEY *(drinks off his drink)*. And speaking of death, I once had a little girl very like you, my honeycake.

GINGER. Yeah I know. But she isn't dead.

STANLEY *(polite)*. Oh is she not? Nobody told me. In any case, the death I refer to wasn't hers . . . although she was there at the time. She and . . . who was it? Who? *(Can't remember. Shakes his head)* However, not a car crash, of that I am positive.

GINGER. What are you talking about now, Grandpa?

STANLEY. Somebody's mother is my recollection though I can't think whose. How did it go? How did it go? My memory's not what it was, you know. Gone right to pot. Hanging was it?

GINGER *(very startled)*. Eh?

STANLEY *(just doddering on)*. No not hanging . . . a woman could never carry a thing like that off properly. Especially not that one. *(Confidential)* Very silly, inefficient woman altogether I'm afraid. And she drank. Now when she telephoned me—

GINGER. Who? The mother?

STANLEY *(testy)*. No, no, no, how could she telephone anybody with her head in the oven. *(Pause)* Or the noose. *(Pause)* Or whatever it was. *(Pause)* Blood? Was there blood? The details have gone clean out of my mind. Isn't that annoying?

GINGER. Grandpa . . .

STANLEY. Well be that as it may this little girl of mine . . . **she** telephoned. Well I say little. She must have been in her teens by then . . . and disgustingly overweight. Why don't you get some of it sliced off I used to say to her. Go along to a butcher, I'd say, nice tender meat. Get a good price for it. If they'll eat whalemeat, they'll eat you . . . Jumbo! *(Laughs. Then irritable again)* Hysterics. Screaming and sobbing down the phone . . . caterwauling . . . oh my goodness. What's all the fuss about I said. Stop being such a fool for once in your life. But she just went bellowing on. I simply rang off.

He stops. Runs his finger round the inside of his glass and licks it. Looks benignly at GINGER.

GINGER.   Go on.

STANLEY.   That's all.

GINGER.   Oh. *(Pause)* Is that a true story?

STANLEY.   I've no idea, precious, no idea at all. *(He gets up out of the deckchair.)* I think I'll be off to bed now.

GINGER.   Wait a minute, Grandpa. Sit down.

STANLEY.   No! Beddy byes! Beddy byes!

GINGER.   I'll give you some more apple juice.

STANLEY *(cheers)*.   Rightyho. *(He sits down again and she fills his glass. He drinks it off).*

GINGER.   Tell me that story again, Grandpa.

STANLEY *(vituperative)*.   She killed her mother.

GINGER *(astonished)*.   What?

STANLEY.   Oh yes! She did! Because she was so fat.

GINGER.   I don't know what you're talking about.

STANLEY *(speeding angrily on)*.   Too fat. Too big. The midwife told me. That baby daughter of yours was too much for her, she said. Take it away, I said to them. Get it out of here. It's a murderer. So they wrapped it up and took it away. I could hear it squalling and yowling all the way down the drive. *(Then through a huge yawn)* I wish you could have seen the flowers, my cherub. Oh mountains of flowers. Cushions made out of white carnations! Hearts made out of red roses . . . would you believe that?

GINGER.   Grandpa . . . *(He leans back in the deckchair and closes his eyes.)*

STANLEY *(sing song. Almost lackadaisical)*.   And then I was all alone. I locked all the doors and all the windows and I pulled all the curtains and I turned off all the lights and then I was all alone. In the dark. Poor lonely one in the dark. *(And he nods off.)*

GINGER.   Wake up, Grandpa. *(Shakes him)* Grandpa, don't go to sleep! *(She looks at him angrily. Then shouts in his ear.)* Wake up! I want to hear the story! *(No response at all. Frustrated)* Nobody ever tells me anything. *(Sulky)* Crazy old bastard.

She snatches the notebook out of STANLEY'S *lap and opens it. She stands between* RAYMOND *and* BABA *as she reads.*

GINGER & BABA *(in unison)*.   Of course you didn't.

BABA.   Of course not. The car crash killed her. It's a miracle it didn't kill you.

RAYMOND.   I'm a miracle?

BABA *(affectionate)*.   You're an egomaniac.

RAYMOND.   In that case dear old Eli probably is my father.

BABA.   You know something?

GINGER *(to herself)*.   No. No. Wait a minute. Where's that other bit? *(Flips through pages)* Oh yeah. Yeah. This is it.

GINGER & RAYMOND *(in unison)*. I heard you! If he is my son.

BABA *gets up at once and goes out as* JOE *comes in.* GINGER *moves to the mattress and settles down to read.* RAYMOND *and* ELI *stand facing each other.*

RAYMOND.   **If.** *(Melodramatic)* Is he my son? *(Pause. Spiteful)* Well I'm not. I've always known I couldn't be . . . Eli! What a fool she was to marry you. You're so boring and pompous and such a drag. No wonder she was unfaithful to you. Who wouldn't be? What was he like, Eli? What was my real father like? Go on, go on . . . tell me.

JOE *(with angry zest)*.   Right! I will, I bloody well will! If your real father is dead, which I devoutly hope he is, he was very talented and very successful and a drunk. He was also my boss and I disliked him intensely. If, on the other hand, your real father is alive, and I pray daily that he is not, I am he. Annie was not unfaithful to anyone. The infidelity in question was between myself and my boss's very neurotic wife. Who was your mother and is also dead. *(Loud)* Are you listening to me, Golden Boy?

RAYMOND *(tense)*.   I'm listening.

JOE.   There was a car crash. He was drunk and she was eight months pregnant with you. Possibly by him or possibly by me although by that time the affair between us had been over for some time and I was in fact engaged to Annie. After the crash you were posthumously delivered by caesarian and kept alive in an incubator. I informed Annie of the possible . . . connection and we adopted you. So now you know! And *(as he goes out of the room)* you're going to board at your school! (RAYMOND *watches him go, expressionless. Then suddenly laughs.*)

RAYMOND *(amiable)*.   God he's funny . . . he's so funny. He really thinks I didn't know all that. *(Gets up and moves around a bit. Sighs)* I wish Mr Albarian was still here. *(Pause)* He thought I was good, he really did. At first I thought he didn't because when I finished playing I looked at him and he was laughing. Sitting there shaking away like a jelly and laughing. But then he patted me on the shoulder a lot of times. *(Slight accent)* How fortunate you are. How fortunate. *(Pause)* He looks you right in the eyes when he's talking to you. Not many people do that. *(Pause)* He wasn't worried about my driving. As a matter of fact I drove impeccably. I went quite slow and I waited for the green every time. *(Pause)* I asked him if he had any children. Seven, he said. Seven! *(Then shouts)* Listen Mr Albarian, your children don't know what it's like. Seven of them! They could all get into the same bed together at night if they wanted to. They'd always have somebody to—

BABA *(as* ANNIE) *has come on and is standing, listening, at a distance. Now, interrupting* RAYMOND, *she mimes knocking on a door and stamps her foot for the sound of the knocks.*

BABA.   Raymond? Raymond!

RAYMOND *(tense)*.   What?

BABA.   Who are you talking to in there?

RAYMOND.   Nobody. *(Shouts angrily)* Nobody! There's nobody here and I'm not talking to anybody. I wish there was. Maybe they'd tell me what I'm supposed to do!

BABA. Why is the door locked? Raymond, what are you—

STANLEY *(sudden. Loud)*. Where is she? *(He gets up. BABA goes off one side and RAYMOND the other.)*

GINGER. Who?

STANLEY *(looks at her, puzzled)*. I don't know. *(Nervous)* Who are you?

GINGER. What do you mean? I'm Ginger.

STANLEY *(unbelieving)*. Who?

GINGER. Ginger. Your granddaughter.

STANLEY *(taken aback)*. My . . . no no. How could I have a granddaughter? I never had any children.

GINGER. Yes you did. You had my— *(breaks off, warning)* Grandpa . . . don't start doing it to me.

STANLEY. No no no no no. No children. Didn't deserve them. That's what they . . . she . . . *(Looks anxiously around the room)* Where is **she**?

GINGER. Who?

STANLEY *(pitifully)*. So angry with me. *(Fiercely)* You don't deserve to have a child at all, she said. *(Looks round the room again)* Who . . .? *(Fierce again)* You don't deserve to have a child at all! *(He sways slightly and moans. GINGER, alarmed, goes to him.)*

GINGER. You okay, Grandpa?

STANLEY. I'd like to lie down. I've got a headache. Would you help me to lie down, little girl? *(He starts to move toward the mattress.)*

GINGER. No, not in here. I'll take you upstairs. Come on.

STANLEY *(quavering)*. Oh dear oh dear oh dear, I'm so tired.

GINGER. Come on, Grandpa. You'll be okay. Come on. *(They reach the door and she looks searchingly at him.)* You do know I'm Ginger, don't you? You do.

STANLEY *(smiles weakly at her)*. Ginger pickle . . . ginger beer . . . gingerbread . . . ginger—

GINGER. Oh my God, there's the front door! Quick. Quick, Grandpa!.

STANLEY *(querulously as they go)*. I want to lie down.

GINGER *(offstage)*. You're going to . . . in a minute. Go on. Up those stairs. Up.

She shuts the door behind them. There is a pause. Then from a little distance NELLY'S voice calling.

NELLY. Baba? *(closer)* Baba are you up there? *(She comes through the door, looks, then calls back through the door.)* No. *(She comes into the room and looks round.)* Good heavens.

JOE comes in. They are both in party clothes and both slightly drunk.

JOE. No? Well, she's probably gone straight up to — *(breaks off)* For God's sake what's all this? *(GINGER appears at the door.)*

GINGER. Hello dad.

JOE. Dad?

GINGER. Just feeling conventional.

JOE.   Ginger, what is all this stuff in here?

GINGER.   My stuff. *(Pause)* My room.

JOE.   Oh God. Sorry, sorry, sorry. Listen have you just been upstairs?

GINGER *(wary)*.   Yes. Why?

JOE.   Is your mother up there?

GINGER.   No. *(Then mocking)* What's the matter? Have you lost her?

JOE *(irritated)*.   Of course not. She left the party before us, that's all.

GINGER.   Well she's not upstairs.

NELLY *(worried)*.   But if she isn't here . . . I mean, where would she go?

JOE.   If I know Baba she probably stopped the taxi halfway home and she's walking the rest of the way. Walking is her sort of — *(breaks off. Listens)* What's that?

GINGER.   What?

JOE.   I can hear something upstairs. *(He starts for the door but GINGER gets there first.)*

GINGER.   It's only the cat. He probably got shut into the spare room. He was up there. I'll go. *(And goes. We hear her voice disappearing)* Puss puss puss. Puss?

JOE *(surveying the room)*.   Baba's not going to be very pleased. *(He wanders over to the mattress and looks at the toys.)* Well, well. Haven't seen these chaps for a few years. The lost tribe, eh?

NELLY.   Joe, do you think we should go and look for Baba?

JOE.   No, that'd probably just annoy her more. Question is . . . what did we do wrong?

NELLY.   We!

JOE *(annoyed)*.   Oh come on, Nelly. I've already told you. I was not drunk and Baba was not angry with me because she thought I was!

NELLY.   How can you be so sure?

JOE.   Because that's not her kind of thing at all.

NELLY.   Last time I was here . . . *(she stops.)*

JOE.   Yes? Last time you were here what?

NELLY.   Well you did get awfully drunk that night, Joe.

JOE *(hackles)*.   Did I?

NELLY.   And you had a horrible row with the twins and Baba was terribly upset. Maybe you don't remember.

JOE *(angry now)*.   Christ . . . ten years ago! Yes I do remember, actually. One of the things I remember is that we were all fairly drunk that night. And everybody ended up in a rage with everybody else except you and Baba of course. Up till dawn crying on each other's shoulders and psychoanalysing me or whatever the hell you were doing.

NELLY.   I only—

JOE.   All right! Ten years ago I used to drink too much. I don't drink too much now.

NELLY.   Joe, I really didn't mean to—

JOE.   Life goes on, Nelly, things happen, things change. Dear God, deliver me from the best friend fantasy.

NELLY.   What do you mean?

JOE.   I mean this naïve obsession you and Baba have that you know each other better than anyone else in the world. You don't. How could you? You don't meet for years on end, you hardly ever write to each other . . . I mean when you were young, yes by all means. Twin souls, alter egos, whatever . . . but now let's face it, it's all a . . . I don't know . . . just a sort of ritual.

NELLY.   It isn't!

JOE.   I'll tell you what it's like. It's like Ginger . . . *(indicates toys)* and these.

NELLY.   Oh for God's sake.

JOE.   No I mean it. When she was young they were inseparable, this lot and Ginger. Slept with her, ate with her . . . she wouldn't go out of the house without taking at least one of them with her. I really think she was closer to them than to anybody. She used—

NELLY *(half joking)*.   Are you calling me a teddy bear?

JOE.   No, I'm calling you a relic from the past. You for Baba . . . Baba for you.

NELLY *(annoyed)*.   I think you must be jealous.

JOE.   Yes I probably am. Yes you're right. Jealous of the completely uncomplicated relationship. Total everything . . . trust, acceptance, approval, support you name it. No daily wear and tear, no annual M.O.T., absolutely no expense on either side.

NELLY.   Really Joe, you—

JOE.   Listen Nelly, I live with Baba . . . the person, not the idea of the person or the memory of the person. And yes there are times when I find it very irritating, you two busily perpetuating the myth that somewhere in the world there is someone who really knows the real you. Someone who understands your every thought, who knows exactly how you feel about absolutely everything. Well there isn't and there never was! It's what everybody wants and nobody gets. It is not part of the deal from the great pack of cards above and it's simply childish and stupid to—

NELLY *(upset)*.   Joe! What did I do? Why are you so angry? *(Stopped in his tracks, he looks at her.)*

JOE *(contrite)*.   Sorry. Sorry, Nelly. *(Goes to her and puts his arms round her)* It's not you I'm angry at, it's Baba. Sorry I shouted. *(He kisses her lightly on the lips. She puts her arms round his neck and kisses him back not lightly. After the kiss)* Wow. Gosh. *(Laughs)* Strong stuff, this . . . the wife's best friend, eh?

NELLY *(moves away. Teasing)*.   Don't be silly. That was a sisterly kiss.

JOE *(moving after her)*.   Oh yes? Well I've always been crazy about incest . . . *(He gets hold of her. She breaks away.)*

NELLY *(sharp)*.   Don't!

JOE *(waggish)*.   What's this? Say no to Big Brother? *(He reaches for her again.)*

NELLY *(angry)*.   Stop it, Joe! You're being ridiculous!

JOE *(exasperated)*.   I'm being! Look Nelly, I wasn't the one—

NELLY *(interrupting. Airily)*.   Right. Absolutely. Point taken. All my fault. Just a bad habit of mine. Get a little drunk . . . make a pass at the nearest man. Any one will do.

JOE *(disgruntled)*.   Thanks a million. *(He shrugs, annoyed and baffled. Then he catches sight of the Calvados.)* Bloody hell! *(Picks up the bottle)* I will kill that girl! *(He goes to the door, opens it and shouts.)* Ginger!

GINGER *(offstage)*.   What?

JOE.   Come here! *(Pause)* Ginger!

GINGER *(offstage)*.   I'm coming I'm coming. *(She appears in the doorway.)* What's up, Doc?

JOE.   Will you please tell me what this is doing in here?

GINGER *(sulky)*.   I just had a little drink.

JOE.   Do you have any idea how much this costs for Christ's sake? *(Checks bottle)* Little!

GINGER.   I gave Grandpa some.

JOE.   What! He's not supposed to have alcohol! Are you out of your mind? It makes him even nuttier, you know that. By God, Ginger —

GINGER.   He was all right. He was fine.

JOE.   I'll bet. By your standards, maybe. You have no sense of responsibility whatever. I would have thought that even you —

GINGER *(very aggrieved)*.   He said he wouldn't go back to the Home unless I gave him a drink. It isn't easy taking care of Grandpa, you know. What was I supposed to do? Let him stay the night?

JOE.   No. *(Pause)*. No. All right, all right. You got him a minicab back?

GINGER.   Yes.

JOE.   Did you telephone them?

GINGER.   Course. I talked to the Matron. I told her what a great time Grandpa had with me at the zoo this afternoon. Matron likes me.

JOE.   She would. *(To* NELLY*)* Matron is the reincarnation of Ghengis Khan. *(Then nodding at* GINGER*)* How do you box ears?

NELLY *(who has sat down. Laughs)*.   I don't know. I've never done it.

JOE.   Come downstairs and have some of this. *(Holds up bottle)* It's extremely good. I was saving it for Armageddon.

NELLY.   Let's stay here. *(Stretches)* I can't move.

JOE.   Right. I'll go down and get some glasses.

GINGER.   I'll get them shall I?

JOE *(suspicious)*.   What's this? Miss Manners is it?

GINGER.   No. Just Daddy's little darling. *(She curtsies to him, finger under chin and goes.)*

JOE *(sits on the toybox)*.   Oh dear. I suppose I should have horsewhipped her or something. There are times when I think what I'm really best at is evading.

NELLY.   The armadillo in the attic.

JOE.   What?

NELLY.   Nothing. *(Pause)* Why did you say you were angry at Baba? What about?

JOE *(grim.)*   Adultery.

NELLY *(amazed)*.   What? Baba?

JOE.   Yes Baba! With her bloody play. *(Half joking)* A novel would have been so much more discreet. I'll be a laughing stock.

NELLY.   Well well. Dear old liberal Joe. Baba was right.

JOE.   Baba is never right. *(Pause)* What about?

NELLY. You not approving of her doing something of her own.

JOE *(annoyed)*. Rubbish. *(Pause. Looks at her)* It's not 'not approve', it's— *(Breaks off. Pause. Then factually)* I get this feeling that I don't matter very much. *(Pause. Interested)* I obviously **am** drunk. Maybe you were right about Baba tonight.

NELLY *(gets up and moves around restlessly)*. I wish she'd come back.

JOE. She will. Walking back to happiness ho ho.

NELLY *(looks at him)*. Do you ever think she might walk out altogether?

JOE *(brisk)*. Not really, no. I doubt if her superego would let her. *(Pause. Smiles at her)*. Apart from which she knows I would fall to pieces if she did.

NELLY. Would you?

JOE. Oh yes.

NELLY *(after a pause)*. I used to toy with the idea myself. Just walking out. *(Bright)* Then the Grim Reaper intervened.

JOE *(startled)*. I always thought you and Ronnie were very happy.

NELLY. Oh we were, we were. Never a cross word. *(Pause)* And all that.

JOE *(slightly embarrassed)*. Of course he **was**—

NELLY. Old.

JOE. Well . . . older.

NELLY *(bright again)*. Twenty-seven years. *(Restless)* The thing about Ronnie was that he cared so much about me. I couldn't believe it was true. He really seemed to think I was what you might call perfect. He was always so kind and so protective and so reliable . . . and so dull. *(Angry)* I hate myself when I do that! *(Turns to* JOE) Do you know I feel irritated with Ronnie for being dead? Irritated. Because you're not allowed to say unkind things about dead people. How's that for bereavement, eh?

JOE *(going toward her)*. Nelly . . . (GINGER *comes in with the glasses,* JOE *takes them.*) Thanks, Ginger. Now buzz off will you. Nelly and I are talking.

GINGER. Ever so sorry, Auntie Eleanor, in the way again am I? *(Pause)* I don't like to seem pushy or anything but this is actually my room.

JOE. All right . . .

NELLY. No no, we mustn't upset the little one. We're the ones who should buzz off. Leave you to your . . . *(nods at toys)* friends.

GINGER *(scoops up two toys. Exaggerated sentiment)*. My **best** friends! *(Holds them up)* Like you and my mummy!

JOE *(handing glass)*. Here you are, Nelly.

NELLY. Oh thank you. Isn't Ginger going to have some? More?

GINGER. No ta, I think it's disgusting. I've got a coke. *(Takes a can out of her pocket. Opens it. Drinks)* Cheers.

JOE. Cheers Nelly.

NELLY. Cheers. *(Swigs. Gasps)* Jesus Mary and Joseph that is strong! (GINGER *laughs*) There now. A merry laugh from the younger generation. How terribly nice. *(She smiles graciously at* GINGER) We were just talking about Ronnie. My husband . . . who you won't remember.

GINGER. I do. He gave me this. *(Holds up toy)*

NELLY. Did he? *(Pause)* So he did.

GINGER.   I liked him, he was terrific. He always called me Miss Rogers.

JOE.   Why?

GINGER *(scathing)*.   Ginger Rogers.

JOE *(mild)*.   I'm just a dunderhead.

GINGER.   I'll drink to that. *(Smiling, they toast each other. NELLY watches them.)*

NELLY *(after a pause)*.   Why can't you be nice to your mother, Ginger?

GINGER *(angry)*.   Because she isn't nice to me! *(Pause. Pleasant)* If it's any of your bloody business.

JOE.   Ginger.

NELLY.   It's quite all right. *(Regards GINGER for a moment. Then sips her drink)* Yes he was smashing, Ronnie. A really nice man in every way. Especially with children. I mean, marvellous with them. Always.

GINGER.   Maybe my mum should have married Ronnie instead of you.

JOE.   Why?

GINGER.   Because she's so childish.

NELLY *(very angry)*.   You little brat!

JOE.   Now, now.

GINGER.   Well she bloody well is sometimes.

NELLY.   Maybe that's because she never got much chance to be childish when she was one. Your grandfather was a mean vicious sod to her when she was a child.

GINGER.   I don't believe it. It's only since he's got old and bonkers that he's mean to her. She's never said anything like that about him to me.

NELLY.   That's because she didn't want to make any of you children hate him. Anyway he shot off to Canada in a rage when she married Joe so she didn't think you'd ever meet him. But you can take it from me that he was always mean to her. He never really wanted her in the first place and he was a hateful father. I know! I was there! He never stopped nagging her and criticising her . . . sending her up, putting her down, humiliating her in front of other people He called her Jumbo! He made her life a misery. He didn't deserve to have a child at all!

GINGER *(startled)*.   Wait a minute! Jumbo?

NELLY *(fierce)*.   No you wait a minute, Ginger and I'll tell you a story about your mother. When we were both thirteen and yes! Best friends. *(Pause. Then goes on with a kind of rapid aggression)* One afternoon we came home to my house after school. Baba was terribly fond of my mother who was, I suppose, a rather foolish woman . . . but certainly lovable. I was quite fond of her myself, actually. By that time my parents were separated but what I didn't know was my mother had a letter that day from my father saying he wanted a divorce. *(Pause. Then on again fast)* It was July and it was a very hot day. She wasn't at home and we decided to wash each other's hair. Which is how we found her. Lying in the bathtub full of blood. And water too, naturally. And she was dead. Also drunk as it turned out later. Cut her wrists . . . not very well but well enough. The thing was we didn't know whether or not she **was** dead. It was quite difficult getting her out of the bath. She kept slipping out of our hands and the blood and the water was splashing all over the place and soaking us. We kept shouting directions to each other at the tops of our voices . . . about how to lift her, get hold of her. When we finally did get her out we could see that she was dead and then we *(a sort of blank pause. Then she goes on tiredly)* started crying and screaming and Baba telephoned her father for help and he . . . hung up on her. *(She stops, not looking at* GINGER *who has been frozen, listening.)*

GINGER *(very upset)*.　Jesus Christ . . .

NELLY *(looks at her. Then ashamed)*.　I shouldn't have told you all that. I'm sorry, Ginger.

GINGER.　No, I . . . *(she makes an awkard gesture)* I am.

NELLY *(vivacious)*.　Your father's heard that story before . . . a lot of times. Nelly's trauma. Nelly's late night in her cups party piece. Sorry to be boring, Joe. Blame the vernal equinox punch at the party.

JOE *(embarrassed)*.　Don't be silly.

The door opens and BABA *comes in wearing party clothes and carrying her coat.*

NELLY.　Baba!

BABA *(stops)*.　Oh. I didn't think you were back.

JOE.　Well as soon as Sandy told us you'd gone off in a taxi in a huff or do I mean in a huff in a taxi, we called another taxi and steamed after you. We thought.

NELLY.　Where did you go?

BABA.　I stopped the taxi halfway and walked home. (JOE *laughs. She glares at him.*) Why is that funny? And what's all this junk doing in here.

GINGER *(slightly shamefaced)*.　I brought it in.

BABA *(unpleasant)*.　I can't think why but I guessed that.

NELLY.　Have a drink, Baba. We're having Joe's priceless Calvados. (BABA *looks at her briefly.*)

BABA.　No thanks. *(Turns back to* GINGER) I'm really terribly sorry about using your room without your permission.

GINGER *(awkward gesture again)*.　Oh listen . . . it's . . .

BABA.　No, no I mean it. I hope you can forgive me for having the temerity to move your things. Inexcusable I do see that now. Me **touching** your precious possessions. Laying a finger on your *(nods at the toys)* sacred objects. How could I have **dared** to be so—

GINGER *(exasperated to* NELLY).　See?

BABA *(whips round. To* NELLY).　See what?

NELLY *(taken aback)*.　Nothing. It was just—

BABA.　Oh yes? *(Back to* GINGER, *openly angry now)* I'd just like to remind you that the last time we had a conversation if that's what you can call you screaming down the phone at me you did say that your intention was never to darken our doors again or lighten our darkness or whatever it is you think you do and—

GINGER.　Oh for Christ's sake, can't you—

BABA.　No I can't and I'd also like to point out that we pay the rates for this house and all the bills . . . well not **we** of course . . . how stupid of me . . . you father. I am just a parasite in a pinny as everybody knows. However, as resident parasite I have a perfect right to use any room in this house for any—

JOE.   Calm down, Baba.

BABA.   Why? Give me one good reason. I am surrounded by people laughing at me.

NELLY *(laughing)*.   Oh Baba . . .

BABA.   Exactly.

NELLY.   What is this?

JOE.   Baba, you do realise we have no idea what you're so upset about. We don't even know why you stormed out of the party.

BABA.   You see? That's typical . . . stormed out. I didn't. I just left. Why does everything I do have to be **absurd.**

NELLY.   It isn't. Why are you —

BABA.   Nelly, I heard you.

NELLY.   What do you mean?

BABA.   At the party. Talking about my play to those people. *(Real hurt)* People I hardly even **know**. Telling them all about it and laughing at me. 'Oh you mustn't call it a hobby for Baba . . . it's a vocation!'

NELLY *(flustered)*.   I didn't mean . . . you know I —

BABA *(interrupting)*.   You're the first person I told . . . I mean the first close person. You're the only one I really wanted to tell . . . Well maybe you're right, maybe I did want Joe to know about it but the reason I hadn't actually told him was because I was afraid he'd think it was silly and then it's you! You're the one!

NELLY.   Baba, I do not think it's silly, not in any way I swear!

BABA.   You can say that now but you didn't know I was listening at the party did you? *(Near tears)* And the worst thing about it is yes it was like a vocation in a stupid sort of way.

GINGER *(embarrassed. Attempting lightness)*.   Some punch that must have been at that party!

JOE.   Shut up, Ginger!

GINGER *(backing away)*.   Sorry . . . sorry . . . only a joke. *(And sits on the mattress.)*

NELLY *(moving towards BABA)*.   Baba please don't be —

BABA *(evading her)*.   Only a joke. Absolutely. That's the story of my bloody life.

JOE *(goes to her. In spite of himself he is smiling)*.   Now Baba, listen . . .

BABA.   I won't. *(Shakes his hand off)* Look . . . you see? You're laughing too.

JOE.   No! *(But can't help it and does)*

BABA.   Yes! It's automatic. I can't even make a scene without being **comic**! My fault, partly my own fault I know that. When in doubt get them to laugh at you it's safer and yes that's what I always used to do. *(To* NELLY*)* But I was serious about this and I thought that you . . . you of all people — *(breaks off)* And there I go sounding like a soap opera.

NELLY *(distressed)*.   If you'd only —

BABA *(overriding. Very dramatic)*.   I don't need any outside help, believe me. I've got enough voices of my own. Inside. Laughing at me all the time. (GINGER *looks up startled. Gets the notebook out from under the mattress and finds a place in it.)* At the things I say, the way I look. What? Self mockery? Self contempt? I'm very good at all that.

GINGER *reads the following line in unison with* BABA *and with* RAYMOND *who comes in saying it.*

BABA/GINGER/RAYMOND.   And of course I have a preternatural gift for paranoia. (BABA *stares at* GINGER. RAYMOND *freezes.*)

BABA.   What are you doing with that? Where did you get it?

GINGER.   I found it.

BABA *(rage)*.   Found!

NELLY.   Ginger!

JOE.   Give that to me.

BABA *(lofty. Calm)*.   It doesn't matter. I don't mind if she reads it. I don't mind who does. I'm throwing it away.

GINGER.   Why?

BABA.   Because it isn't any good. As I'm sure you'll agree.

GINGER.   Well if you think that, how come you were quoting from it?

BABA *(fast. Childish)*.   I wasn't.

GINGER.   You were too! *(Pointing at the page)* Right here. This—

JOE.   Ginger will you just shut up! Look Baba, I know how you feel . . .

BABA.   No. You don't. *(She starts for the door.* NELLY *follows her.)*

NELLY.   Wait!

BABA *(rather violently)*.   Leave me alone, Nelly!

She slams out. GINGER *goes up to the door and shouts.*

GINGER.   You're crazy to throw it away. It's good!

NELLY *stands still for a moment and then walks back and sits on the toybox. Sits preoccupied and unaware of the following.* JOE *goes to get the book from* GINGER.

JOE.   Give it to me, Ginger.

GINGER *(dancing away from him)*.   No. Wait a minute. Let me read a little bit of it to you.

JOE.   Certainly not.

GINGER *(evading him again and getting behind a chair)*.   Oh come on, just a little bit. She said she didn't mind who read it.

JOE.   Give it to me **now.** *(Reaching for it again)* I'm going to take it to Baba.

GINGER *(getting away from him)*.   Oh Joe, you just don't know anything about women.

JOE *(stung)*.   What?

GINGER.   She wants to be left alone. She's probably having a nice cry.

JOE *(again laughs in spite of himself)*.   Ginger you are a terrible person!

GINGER.   I know, I know. Now listen to this . . . you will be amazed. I'm not kidding. I don't know why she didn't tell me. You'd think she'd be proud of it. Really . . . I mean! Who would've ever thought she could! Listen. Please?

JOE.   All right, all right, all right. *(He sits)*

GINGER & RAYMOND *(in unison)*.   What? Self mockery? Self contempt?

RAYMOND.   I'm very good at all that. And of course I have a preternatural gift for paranoia.

BABA *comes in as* ANNIE *from the wings wearing the dressing-gown of Act One.*

BABA. Preternatural paranoia . . . well it alliterates.

RAYMOND. If he'd said that I would have wanted to smash his face in.

BABA. Well, he's your father.

RAYMOND. Or not.

BABA. I'm not talking about biology. Whether or not you sprang from his actual loins he is your father. The father person in your life since you were five weeks old. Whereas I have to share the parental honours with an incubator.

RAYMOND. And a corpse.

BABA *(starts to go).* Oh well if it's going to be one of those conversations.

RAYMOND Don't go. I'm sorry.

BABA. Showing off again.

RAYMOND. I can't help it if I've got a mordant wit.

BABA. You just enjoy shocking people.

RAYMOND. I don't particularly enjoy it. It's really just a habit.

BABA. That's worse. *(There is a pause.)*

RAYMOND *(hesitant).* Mother?

BABA. Yes?

RAYMOND *(passion).* It wasn't my fault! I didn't kill her.

BABA. Of course you didn't. Of course not. The car crash killed her. It's a miracle it didn't kill you.

RAYMOND. I'm a miracle?

BABA *(affectionate).* You're an egomaniac.

RAYMOND. In that case dear old Eli probably is my father.

BABA. You know something? You're not so much tiresome as tiring.

RAYMOND. I know. But remember it's tiring for me too. It's hard work being eccentric and highly strung. There are times when I wish I'd opted for thick but endearing. Yours is nice.

BABA. My what?

RAYMOND. Your cover. And not particularly tiring either, I shouldn't think. Amiable, placid, patient, gentle, *(smiles)* . . . nice.

BABA. Raymond, people don't have 'covers' . . . they have personalities.

RAYMOND. Though mind you it must be quite exhausting keeping the real you out of sight sometimes. With him for example. Eli. The maybe father maybe not. I bet there are times when you'd like to give him a swift kick in the goolies, eh?

BABA *(half laugh).* Raymond!

RAYMOND *(laughs too).* It's what our P.E. teacher says. Would you like a swift kick in the goolies, boy? Weird way of putting it, really. What does he expect us to say? *(Eager)* Oh yes please sir! I'd really like that, sir.

BABA. *(trying not to laugh).* Why do you think people should have 'covers'?

RAYMOND *(surprised).* To hide their real selves.

BABA. Oh yes? Well what do you think the real me is like.

RAYMOND.   Oh. Well . . . um . . . arrogant, aggressive, domineering, ruthless, intolerant . . . and a terrible cook.

BABA *(indignant)*.   I'm a good cook!

RAYMOND.   Ah but that's just your cover. *(She laughs. They smile at each other.)*

BABA *(after a pause)*.   I want to tell you something.

RAYMOND.   What?

BABA.   I'm going to have a baby. *(There is a longish pause. Then carefully)* And the way I see it you can either have a nervous breakdown or be glad. *(Another pause)*.

RAYMOND *(conversational)*.   When it's born, I'll kill it.

GINGER.   Isn't that brilliant? *(She shuts the book and BABA and RAYMOND go off.)* I think it's great. When it's born I'll kill it. Terrific. He's a real poncey little creep, this Raymond. Well so's the one called Eli. The father. He's very depressed all the time and amazingly boring.

JOE.   Oh yes?

GINGER.   Yeah . . . a real wanker. And I'll tell you something else! Mr Albarian's in it. You know . . . the geezer at the newsagent down the road. The little fat one. He's a really nice man. She's just pinched him and put him in her play. Hasn't even changed his name. She's made him into a piano tuner. What's he going to think when he sees it!

JOE *(alarmed)*.   You're not going to show it to him.

GINGER *(surprised)*.   No on the stage I mean . . . when he sees it in the theatre.

JOE.   Oh.

GINGER *(flipping pages)*.   I'll read you the beginning of it, shall I?

JOE *(grabbing the notebook)*.   No!

GINGER *(aggrieved)*.   What's the matter? Don't you like it? Don't you think it's good?

JOE *(brusque)*.   Yes. As a matter of fact I do.

GINGER.   Well then. (JOE *puts the notebook in the drawer of the writing table.)*

NELLY *(getting up)*.   I'm going to find Baba.

JOE.   I expect she's just gone up to bed, you know.

GINGER *(galvanised)*.   Up to . . .? Oh my God!

She rushes to the door. When she opens it BABA, in her party dress, nearly falls into the room.

GINGER.   You've been listening! *(Delighted laughter)* Eavesdropping!

BABA *(lofty)*.   I simply came back to get my coat.

NELLY *(moves toward her)*.   Oh Baba, listen . . .

BABA *(loud)*.   Listen!

NELLY *(disconcerted)*.   What?

BABA *(frightened)*.   What's that?

Offstage the sound of a ghostly cat mewing. They all listen as the sounds get louder. STANLEY shuffles into the room with a blanket round his shoulders.

STANLEY. Meow . . . meow . . . meow . . . meow . . . *(He looks at them reproachfully)* I was lonely. I couldn't sleep. I was all alone. *(As he comes further into the room* BABA *backs away apprehensively. He catches sight of her and his face lights up.)* There you are, Barbara. Couldn't think where you'd got to. *(Sees* NELLY*)* Hideyho Nelly, dear. *(He totters over to the deckchair and sits in it)* You waited for me didn't you, old fellow. *(Pats the chair)* I knew you'd wait for me. *(Yawns)* I'll be as right as rain now. Right as rain.

They all watch hypnotised as he closes his eyes and nods off. JOE *turns on* GINGER *who has been backing toward the door.*

JOE. Ginger . . .

BABA. Ssshhhh! *(They all look at* STANLEY *who snores gently.)*

GINGER *(hoarse whisper)*. Well it wasn't my fault. He wanted to go to MacDonald's. And then there weren't any minicabs. What was I supposed to do? *(During which she's got herself through the door.)*

JOE. Come back here. *(He follows her through the door. Offstage).* Ginger . . .

BABA *(low. Looking at* STANLEY*)*. My God! I always said he was putting the whole thing on.

She picks up her coat and starts out. NELLY *grabs her arm. The following is in half-whispers.*

NELLY. Wait.

BABA. What?

NELLY. I'm sorry.

BABA *(pretending not to understand)*. Sorry about what?

NELLY *(irritated)*. You know. What I said at the party.

BABA. Don't worry about it. It doesn't matter.

NELLY. It does. (STANLEY *mutters and stirs. They look at him. He subsides.)*

BABA *(starting out again)*. Please Nelly, just forget all about it.

NELLY. No I won't! Will you stop being so bloody wonderful and forgiving and just listen to me for a minute? *(Startled,* BABA *stops and looks at her.)* I'm sorry. Okay? I really am sorry! I told you I was envious about you and your plays and I am. That's why I was being bitchy and I feel awful about it. And I'm also envious of you having the kind of husband you can fight with and I came all this way to talk to you about how guilty I felt about Ronnie and you didn't want to listen to me.

BABA *(stung)*. I tried! You wouldn't talk about it.

NELLY *(not whispering)*. You should have made me! *(An apprehensive glance at* STANLEY *who slumbers on. She goes on in lower tones.)* You're my best friend. You're the only one who can tell me what to do.

BABA. Do about what?

NELLY *(exasperated)*. My life. The rest of my life!

BABA. Nelly, that's impossible!

NELLY. I know! I know that!

BABA. Well then?

NELLY.   I just **wanted** it to be possible.
BABA *(moving toward her)*.   Oh Nelly . . .
STANLEY *(screams)*.   She's back! The devil's come back!
NELLY.   Oh my God!
BABA.   Dad!
STANLEY.   Help! Help!
NELLY *(going to the door)*.   Joe!
STANLEY.   She'll eat me alive. Help me!
BABA *(furious)*.   Shut up. Just shut up will you!

JOE *and* GINGER *come in.* STANLEY *goes to them.*

STANLEY.   Dr Renfrew! Protect me!
GINGER.   Grandpa cut that out!
STANLEY *(amazed)*.   What?
GINGER.   Leave her alone. You can save all that for Matron. When you
    come to our house you can just behave yourself, I mean that! *(Everyone
    is silent, gazing at* GINGER.)
STANLEY *(pitifully)*.   Barbara?
BABA *(startled)*.   What? *(He shuffles over to her.)*
STANLEY.   You shouldn't let her talk to her grandfather like that. It's
    very rude. I can't sleep, Barbara . . . all this shouting. *(Wheedling)*
    Matron gives me hot chocolate when I can't sleep. Will you make me
    some hot chocolate?
JOE *(taking his arm)*.   Come on, Stanley. I'll make you some.
STANLEY *(as he's led out)*.   Oh how wonderfully kind of you.
JOE *(as they go)*.   What's my name?
STANLEY.   Joe. Short for Joseph. My goodness me don't you remember
    your own name! Dear, dear, dear . . .

GINGER, *not looking at* BABA *and* NELLY, *scoops up the cuddly toys,
drops them into the toybox, letting the lid drop with a bang and starts out of
the room dragging the mattress.*
NELLY *and* BABA *watch her go as the lights fade and the music of the Cello
Concerto comes up.*

The Committee

Characters

NANNY
SECRETARY
EXAMINER

First performed at the Cockpit Theatre in a programme of short plays commissioned by John Halle and called *Fireworks*.

NANNY	Bernard Hopkins
THE EXAMINER	Ian White
MISS SPRING	Jill Dixon

Directed by Michael Hucks.

THE COMMITTEE

They come on into the dark. Very old fashioned NANNY in long black dress and white pinny, lame and walks with a stick and carries a hamper basket. The EXAMINER dressed in morning suit. The SECRETARY in black-and-white striped shirt, longish black skirt, heavy rimmed glasses, shorthand notebook and pen.
The EXAMINER has a bunch of sparklers in one hand and a lighted one in the other. He leads the way and as one sparkler starts to go out he lights another from it. The SECRETARY follows immediately behind him and NANNY shuffles along behind her. NANNY is a man.

NANNY.   Look! Look!
SECRETARY *(controlled nervous start)*.   Where? What do you mean?
EXAMINER.   It doesn't matter. Could you find the light switch, Miss Spring.
SECRETARY.   Of course. *(Immediately turns on light)*

The EXAMINER lets the sparkler go out and sits on a swivel chair, centre. Puts the other sparklers on the floor beside him.

NANNY *(disappointed)*.   Is that all?
EXAMINER.   That's all for the moment.
NANNY *(sits on basket)*.   Well I don't call that much of a show. Wouldn't have come if I'd known. I'm an old woman. Junketting about for the sake of a few measly sparklers. *(Clasps her hand and inclines toward imaginary child sitting at her feet)* Oh dearie, I remember the day, long before you was born, the King and Queen, their Majesties, up on their balcony. The Palace.

SECRETARY sits on small chair at the side and starts taking shorthand.
EXAMINER faces out absolutely still and expressionless.

NANNY.   Oh, with the lovely little princesses and the old Queen, a great lady she was God rest her. The fireworks then! Pictures in the air all made of light and fire! I was standing in the crowd holding my Jess's arm and I said to him, 'Oh Jess,' I said, 'D'you think I'll ever meet the Queen?' And he said to me and he squeezed my arm, always a gentleman, ever so shy, he said . . .

EXAMINER *(kindly)*.   Thank you Nanny. Did you get that down Miss
  Spring?
SECRETARY.   Yes.
EXAMINER.   Would you be good enough to read it back?
SECRETARY.   Certainly. *(Reads. Calm.)* I was at my typewriter
  working. It was not going well and my deadline was already past. I had
  been to a party the night before and had drunk rather too much.
  Consequently I was feeling a bit sick. The desk was littered with papers,
  unanswered letters, unpaid bills. None of the beds were made. I got up
  several times and looked searchingly at myself in the mirror and did not
  care for what I saw. It was a grey clammy day and I was a grey and
  clammy person. It was apparent that I had failed in every way and that
  my life was tediously ridiculous but I had neither the wit nor the courage
  nor the *(pauses to make out next word)* interest to terminate my
  existence. Then I heard the voice.
EXAMINER.   I see. Yes. *(Stands and thinks for a moment. Then brisk)*
  Yes. I think we can work from there, why not? Miss Spring you will play
  the protagonist?
SECRETARY *(suddenly frightened)*.   No! No I couldn't!
EXAMINER *(interested)*.   Really not?
SECRETARY *(desperately to* NANNY*)*.   No. I—I—please—I—
NANNY *(lumbering to her feet)*.   Never you mind, my lovey. Nanny'll do
  it. *(To* EXAMINER*)*. With respect, Sir, it's perhaps asking a bit much at
  this stage.
SECRETARY *(prim)*.   I quite agree.
EXAMINER.   Possibly. We'll see. *(Helps* NANNY *to swivel-chair and
  goes upstage standing back to audience)* When you're ready.
NANNY *(in* MISS SPRING'S *tidy delivery)*.   It was coming from some
  distance. Shouting. A woman's voice. That surprised me. I knew it was
  God, naturally, but a woman? *(Straining. Anxious face)* I couldn't hear
  the words . . .
EXAMINER *(through loud-hailer)*.   It is Yahweh who speaks. I will tear
  away your horses from you and destroy your chariots; tear the towns of
  your country from you, bring down all your strongholds; tear the charms
  from your hands and you will have no more soothsayers; tear from you
  your images and your pillars; tear from you your sacred poles and
  demolish your idols; and no longer will you bow down before the work of
  your hands. I will take revenge in anger and fury.
NANNY.   I was stricken with terror. My stomach leapt and flashed with
  panic. It has come, I thought. My punishment. If I could only hear the
  words. So I stood up and I gripped the edge of the desk and I strained to
  hear. 'Speak to me', I said under my breath. I was sweating and shaking
  but I knew I had to hear the words.

EXAMINER *goes to* SECRETARY *and hands her the loudhailer. She
takes it, turns upstage and shouts into it.*

SECRETARY.   Into line everyone. Into line I said. Anderson! Hopkins!
  Stringer! Into line at once. Starting points please everyone. When I blow
  the whistle jump to it. Good luck girls. Now then. On your marks, get set
  — *(she stops abruptly)*.

NANNY *(matter of fact)*.   It was only the Sports day at the school down the road.

EXAMINER.   You felt relieved.

NANNY.   No. Foolish.

EXAMINER. How? In what way?

NANNY.   Presumptuous.

EXAMINER.   I don't understand.

NANNY *(sighs. Then in a monotone)*.   Why would God speak to you, I thought. Who do you think you are?

SECRETARY *(sits. Flips through notebook. Reads in a businesslike way)*. The room suddenly full of people.

NANNY.   Laughing. Mocking me.

EXAMINER.   Who? What people?

NANNY.   Parents. Prefects. Bank Managers. Shop assistants.

SECRETARY *(reads)*.   Cardinals. Movie stars. Political prisoners. Explorers. Prophets.

NANNY.   Starving babies. Nuns.

SECRETARY.   Martyrs. *(Snaps book shut)*.

EXAMINER.   It seemed to you neither reasonable nor probable that God should address you. Personally?

NANNY *(yawns)*.   I felt exposed. Ridiculous.

EXAMINER *(to SECRETARY)*.   Is there further data?

SECRETARY *(finding place in book)*.   Yes. One letter dated March 1st, 1929. 'Thanking you for yours of the 14th ultimo, I must inform you in reference to your question in paragraph two that I have never been eminent or well-known *(pause to make out next words)* to anyone. As far as I can discover from my files I have never in my lifetime, experienced any crucial suffering or severe or important *(pause to make out word)* pain'.

NANNY *(moving back to basket)*.   Not true, my pet, not true. Nanny remembers. What about the night you came in to me in your little white nightie. All pale and shaky, trying not to cry. 'Oh Nanny', you said, 'Oh Nanny', and you couldn't say nothing else. Only seven you were, not more. And her *(bitter)* out swanking with her literary friends. Out of bed I jumped. 'What is it my precious?' I said. 'Tell Nanny', and you sat in my lap and I rocked you and rocked you and I sang you a little song.

EXAMINER *(sits in swivel-chair. Talks song)*.   Sail baby, sail, out across the sea, only don't forget to sail, back again to me.

SECRETARY *gets up slowly, hands notebook and pen to EXAMINER, also her glasses which he puts on. She walks over to NANNY and sits crosslegged beside her. EXAMINER takes notes.*

SECRETARY *(young voice)*.   I heard them talking downstairs, the grown-ups. They said when you died you went out like a light. Just like a light. So I tried and tried to think about that, about me going out like a light and I couldn't see how that could happen and I got scared and my legs started jumping in a funny way. What would the world be like if I wasn't in it? If I'd gone out like a light? My room felt full of nothing. Full. *(Stops.)*

NANNY. And then you heard this funny noise . . .

SECRETARY *(nods.)* A rushing. Like the ocean and the wind. And. And. And. *(Stops again. Then fast)* I wanted to scream but I was too embarrassed. They would think I was silly. But I had to do something.

NANNY. A course you did. A course.

SECRETARY. So I got out of my bed and I went to the window. Up in the sky there were a million birds flying in front of the moon. And I said to them in a whisper, 'Help. Help. Help.'

EXAMINER *(rather unpleasantly. Pen poised)*. And then?

SECRETARY *gets up and switches off the light.*

SECRETARY. I refuse to answer the question.

EXAMINER. The . . . narrative, then, has no conclusion?

SECRETARY. None.

EXAMINER. Significance? Consequence?

SECRETARY *(flat)*. No.

EXAMINER. Absolutely no point at all, is that correct?

SECRETARY. That is correct. *(The* EXAMINER *lights a sparkler.)*

NANNY. Wrong? I say wrong!

EXAMINER. Yes?

NANNY. Everything's important, that I do know. My Mum used to say it to me. Everything you do or say matters to the Lord Above, she told me. What about the fall of the sparrow, eh? Answer me that. I know I'm only an old woman and I may be a fool but—

EXAMINER *(agreeable)*. Certainly you are a fool.

NANNY *(violently)*. Don't speak to me like that! Naughty! Wicked! Mustn't be wicked and naughty.

EXAMINER. The light *(*SECRETARY *switches on the light.)*

EXAMINER *(reads)*. I have here that in passing bus queues or cinema queues or even small groups of people standing about on the pavement, I experience the sensation that one of my legs is shorter than the other. Or the other longer. I am aware, intellectually as it were, that my legs are more or less exactly the same length. However it seems impossible to communicate this conviction to the rest of my body. I feel that I am probably limping but because I cannot be positive of this and because all the people are staring at me, I do in fact begin deliberately to limp. Exaggeratedly. This tends to bring a flush of embarrassment to my face and sometimes tears to my eyes. *(Stops.)*

SECRETARY. Go on.

EXAMINER *(clears throat and then continues rapidly)*. The difficulty lies in the decision when to cease limping. Once I have passed the people I cannot be sure how long they may continue to look at me. There is the added hazard that I might encounter someone I know.

SECRETARY. And?

EXAMINER *(shuts book. Takes off glasses)*. There is no more.

NANNY. I say again. Wrong. A little prayer to your Guardian Angel. That's what my poppet did that night. 'Help, Guardian Angel, hear my cry' she said. And she was sent to me and I became the humble vessel for Our Lady, pouring out love and comfort just as she did for our dear Lord Jesus.

EXAMINER *(small boy voice)*.   What have you got in your basket, Nan?

NANNY.   Oh ever so many surprises for a good boy. Lovelies.

EXAMINER *(as before)*.   Show! Show!

SECRETARY *(as child)*.   Please Nanny, please! Do Show us!

NANNY.   Now now, mustn't tease. Will you promise Nanny never to be wicked again?

BOTH.   Promise!

NANNY.   Tidy up your toys? Do your lessons? Empty your bowels every morning after breakfast? Always have a clean hankie?

BOTH. Yes! Promise promise!

NANNY *(coy)*.   Renounce the Devil and all his pomp?

BOTH.   Yes yes yes!

NANNY.   Help me up then. Bring Nanny a chair.

They help her up and the EXAMINER *brings over the small chair. The* SECRETARY *moves the swivel-chair to the side and brings notebook, pen and glasses over to the floor by* NANNY'S *chair.)*

NANNY *(opening basket)*.   Now then, what have we got today? Sit down, there's dears. *(They sit on either side of her)* Yes. That's right. Here's one for you. *(Takes out black savage mask with bone through nose and hands it to the* SECRETARY) Put it on. Put it on. *(She does)* And one for you. *(Takes out beautiful bird mask and hands it to the* EXAMINER *who puts it on)* Now where are those spectacles? I had them just here . . . *(searches basket)* I'll be losing my head next. *(Plaintive)* Who's got Nan's specs, eh? (EXAMINER *hold them up and crows like a rooster)* There's a good girl. And who's the bad boy sitting on Nan's notebook? *(The* SECRETARY *hands her the book and makes a growling noise)* That's Nan's **good** boy. *(While leafing through book speaks absently)* Try and be good children always and when you go to heaven you'll be two little stars in the sky . . . ah. Here we are. *(To* EXAMINER) Find the drum, dear. *(He takes it out of the basket and gives it to her)* Up you get now, my duckies.

They get up and stand facing each other a little distance from her. As she begins to read she beats a rhythm on the drum punctuating the phrases. They perform a simple and rather formal dance to this.

NANNY.   It's always the same. I begin to go down. The life in my face, in my eyes ebbs . . . ebbs. I become prey to a thousand trivial doubts. Like a heavy rotting log I lie with the doubts, a swarm of dull, patient little beetles, crawling over me, through me, inside me. From time to time the terror flares up and sets off thoughts like gun shots. Get up early! Learn French! Lose weight! Phone the dentist! Read the Tibetan Book of the Dead! Weep! Pray! Sing! Howl! *(Then very brightly)* Here comes a candle to light you to bed and here comes a chopper to chop off your head.

They execute a jolly skipping dance to this and she does a roll on the drums.

NANNY.   There we are! Lovely!

Now the SECRETARY *starts stalking the* EXAMINER *like a beast after a bird. He flutters and leaps away and she moves heavily after him. They both make noises.*

NANNY *(watching, head on one side).*   Yes . . . yes . . . very nice . . .

Then the SECRETARY *catches him, puts her arms around him and starts to nuzzle and fondle him, to which he responds with shrill ecstatic cries.*

NANNY *(very agitated).*   Stop it at once, do you hear me. Nanny can't bear that sort of thing. Hateful. Disgusting. Stop! Stop! Stop!

And they stop and take the masks off and put them in the basket. The EXAMINER *puts the drum away and the* SECRETARY *takes the glasses and notebook.* NANNY *sits eyes shut, head up, swaying and moaning. They stand on either side of her looking at her. The* SECRETARY *clears her throat.* NANNY *goes on moaning.*

SECRETARY.   Wake up please. Doctor hasn't much time.
NANNY *(open eyes).*   Wha . . . Who . . . where am I? Where've they taken me?
SECRETARY.   Never mind where you are. You're perfectly safe. Just answer the questions.
EXAMINER.   How long have you had this trouble?
NANNY *(sulky).*   Long as I can remember.
EXAMINER.   Your age?
NANNY.   I don't have to answer that. I know my rights. Bleeding questions. Poking their noses in . . .
EXAMINER.   Buck up please, and pay attention. You have had treatment for the condition?
NANNY.   No, never. I wouldn't. They put you in there . . . do what they want to you. Muck you about with tablets what make you see things. Put wires on your head . . . all woozy for days and you can't remember nothing properly. Cut you! They'd cut you! Oh no. Oh no. I'll stay in my own home thank you. Take care of myself like I always done. Let me out of here! *(Starts to struggle. The* SECRETARY *restrains her)* I want to go home!
EXAMINER *(very sharp).*   That will do. *(She subsides at once).* Have you tried the ordinary home remedies? Tobacco? Television? Transcendental Meditation? Masturbation? Anything of that nature?
NANNY *(bad tempered).*   All. I tried 'em all. Much good.
EXAMINER.   How often do you have a bath?
NANNY *(flailing out).*   That's my private affair. You mind your own business, you. I don't have to . . . I got my pride . . . I
EXAMINER *(interrupting).*   Be quiet. *(She is)* What exactly are the symptoms at this time?
NANNY.   I told you. I told you all that already.
EXAMINER.   Ah yes. *(Motions to* SECRETARY).
SECRETARY *(reads without expression).*   It's always the same. I begin to go down. The life in my face, in my eyes ebbs . . . ebbs. I become prey to a thousand trivial doubts. Like a heavy rotting log I lie with the doubts,

a swarm of dull patient little beetles, crawling over me, through me, inside me. From time to time the terror flares up and sets off thoughts like gun shots. Get up early. Learn French. Lose weight. Phone the dentist. Read the Tibetan Book of the Dead. Weep, pray, sing, howl.
EXAMINER.   Mmmm hmmm. *(Takes notebook and reads.)* Yes well. There isn't much we can do about the beetles I'm afraid. Though as I say regular bathing might alleviate matters. *(Looks thoughtfully at NANNY and then bends and sniffs her)* Pooh! Dear me, some of these people live like pigs. I suppose we could just hose her down. Carbolic. Disinfectant. Shave the head. More lice then beetles I'll be bound. Yes. That might be quite a good notion.

NANNY *lurches* off the chair and crawls over to the SECRETARY *grabbing her round the legs. The* SECRETARY *is expressionless.*

NANNY *(blubbering).*   Oh please Miss, don't let them. I never did nobody no harm. Tell him to let me go. Tell him. Tell him.
SECRETARY *(pushing her away).*   I am not in charge here.
EXAMINER *(laughs heartily).*   Oh my goodness, no. That would be a strange state of affairs. In charge indeed. Self, self, self — that's all you people think about nowadays. Back in the chair please.

The SECRETARY *gets* NANNY *back into the chair.*

EXAMINER *(refers to book).*   Let me see. Mmmm 'pray . . . doubt it. Can be very tricky . . . hmm . . . 'sing' . . . well . . . Yes. Give it a go. Why not? Sing something.

NANNY *sings the first line or so of Isis und Osiris in a very deep rich voice.*

EXAMINER *(cutting her off).*   Thank you. Don't call us, we'll call you. *(Is suddenly overcome with giggles and has difficulty in stopping. Clears throat)* Well. The only course open to us is to fall back on the howling. Would you howl for us please.

NANNY *howls in a formal manner. Looks enquiringly at him.*

EXAMINER.   I see. Rather orthodox. Not much get-up-and-go in that kind of thing. Try again please.

NANNY *tries again but coughs and sputters instead.*

EXAMINER.   No use whatever I'm afraid. Please. *(To* SECRETARY*)* Will you?

The SECRETARY *puts back her head and howls. It is the real thing.*

EXAMINER.   Splendid. That's the ticket. Now then —

But he is interrupted by the SECRETARY *who howls again and again with increasing pain and despair.* NANNY *gets up and she and the* EXAMINER *get the* SECRETARY *into the chair where she sits curled up, shuddering and sobbing.*

NANNY.   Stop it! That's enough silly crying. We've had far too much of that carry-on already. Sit up Miss. Your father wants to hear the truth.

SECRETARY.   No no no!
NANNY.   Do as you're told this minute. Sit up. Behave yourself. Sit up at once.

The SECRETARY *sits up and looks from one to the other apprehensively.*

EXAMINER *(kind. Lethal).*   Now then, Child. No one's going to hurt you. Simply tell me what happened.
SECRETARY.   I didn't do it. Truly truly I didn't. Cross my heart.
NANNY.   Fibs! Wicked fibs! *(To* EXAMINER*)* I didn't like to trouble you, Sir, knowing how busy you are but I thought, No , I thought, this is going too far. This must not pass unnoticed. Oh I've prayed to God for guidance, Sir, believe me I—
EXAMINER.   Quite right, Nanny. Very right and proper that you should bring the matter to me. After all there might have been a possibility of physical danger to my person.
NANNY *(to* SECRETARY *with accusing horror).*   A snake in your daddy's bed! How could you!
SECRETARY.   I didn't! Jess did it! Besides it was only a grass snake. He did it! Jess did!
NANNY *(shock).*   My Jess! He wouldn't be able to imagine such a thing. He wouldn't hurt a hair of his Daddy's head.
EXAMINER.   Quite right, Nanny. This was no boy's mischievous prank. No, no. This was sly, secret, spiteful. *(Right into* SECRETARY's *face)* Revenge! Admit it! Admit that you . . .

NANNY *suddenly turns and walks over to the side of the stage.*

EXAMINER *(off his stroke).*   Where are you going?
NANNY *(sits down).*   I'm tired.
EXAMINER *(urgent).*   Come back! I'm not sure that I can . . . *(whisper)* Help me!
NANNY.   No. *(Puts head on knees and apparently goes to sleep. The* SECRETARY *gets up but the* EXAMINER *pushes her savagely back.)*
EXAMINER *(fast and very incoherent).*   And as for you just one question, answer me that, tell me, help me . . . I mean. *(Deep breath. Carefully)* I want an answer to one question before I punish you . . . *(with relish)* severely for your *(fast)* shocking, ungrateful, disgusting, selfish, evil I say evil behaviour. *(Mounting excitement)* I am not angry, I am not even surprised . . . no, no, no, not surprised. This kind of thing does not come from my side of the family. Could not. Should not. No! Not! *(Pulls back)* Not angry I repeat but disappointed, grieved, bitterly, bitterly hurt *(laughs suddenly. Cut it off).* That she should be . . . resurrected in this dreadful way . . . this, this, this . . . So Moses threw his staff on the ground and it turned into a serpent and he drew back from it . . . I—I—I *(looks desperately at* NANNY. *Then shouts)* Just one question. Why?
SECRETARY *(shouts immediately back at him).*   Love!

The EXAMINER *backs away from her, crouching and covering his ears.*

EXAMINER *(low, tense voice).* How dare you. How could you say such a thing. A child to its . . . a child. Our Father. Your father . . . *(Calls. Frightened)* Father! Father! *(With great effort straightens up and speaks formally)* Its parent. *(Then begins reasonably but becomes excited again)* No it's too much. This even I cannot abide. Fond, devoted, loyal, admiring, honouring — certainly certainly. All these are excellent things in a woman . . . a child . . . yes all . . . a child . . . but to say . . . to dare to say something so . . . so vile! Where's that cane? *(Goes swiftly to basket and takes out a whip)* Ah this will do.

He cracks the whip. NANNY sits up and looks round. The SECRETARY rushes over to him and tries to put her arms around him. He pushes her violently away.

EXAMINER *(cracking the whip).* Don't touch me.
NANNY *(getting to her feet and peering at him, puzzled).* Why not? Why not touch?

The EXAMINER looks confusedly over at her and MISS SPRING seizes the whip from him. He stands dazed.

SECRETARY. Because he's dangerous. Come and help me. Quickly.

NANNY *goes to her and together they take off her shirt and skirt. She is wearing spangled circus costume underneath. The EXAMINER has folded his arms and stands like a statue looking away. The SECRETARY goes to him and during her next speech pushes him about, but he seems impervious. NANNY backs away and watches intently.*

SECRETARY. This is a savage but he doesn't know it. He thinks he's some kind of a king. He wounds, he mauls, he murders. But he's not ashamed of it. In fact he's hardly aware of it. He calls it surviving . . . doing his job . . making a living. He's proud. He's greedy. He cannot love.

At this point the EXAMINER comes to and makes a menacing lunge at her. She leaps back and picks up the small chair in lion-tamer fashion.

SECRETARY *(To NANNY).* Get back ladies and gentlemen, I warn you, get back.

NANNY scuttles to the side of the stage and sits as audience. Now as the SECRETARY speaks she plays the EXAMINER with the chair and the whip while he silently moves about.

SECRETARY *(gipsy like Cockney. Shouts).* Watch him carefully, ladies and gentlemen dear. You think he's quiet eh? You think he's gentle? I tell you he is dangerous in the true sense of the word. King of the jungle! *(Laughs gladly)* Come on my beauty! Come on my bully boy!
NANNY *(as to others in audience).* Cor isn't she brave! Fearless isn't she?
SECRETARY. Never been touched have you? Get back then, get back! I'm not afraid of you. You don't scare me!

She turns her back on him and walks downstage. Stands facing out in a provocative pose with the chair held right out in one hand and the whip in the other. Shouts out.

SECRETARY.   Come on! Touch me! Touch me!

The EXAMINER *crouches for* SPRING, NANNY *leans forward watching in horror. They freeze. Then the* EXAMINER *leaps.*

NANNY *(as he leaps).*   Look! Look!

The SECRETARY *steps aside and he falls on his face on the stage and is still.*

NANNY *(gets up and moves forward warily).*   Is he dead?
SECRETARY *(looking down at him).*   No. Wait. Watch.

He remains still and they are silent watching him. Then he gets up neatly and very calmly walks over and gets the swivel-chair, puts it in its original position, sits, crosses legs. They are silent.

EXAMINER *(not looking at them).*   Is there any further old business?

NANNY *sighs heavily and moves over to her basket. The* SECRETARY *goes to the back and starts putting on her skirt and shirt.*

NANNY *(as she sits. Sadly).*   No.
EXAMINER *(after a pause).*   Is there any new business?

SECRETARY *carries her chair over to its original spot. Sits. She has the notebook, opens it, looks, shuts it.*

SECRETARY.   None.

Blackout.

The Twenty-Second Day

Characters

AUGUSTA
THOMAS
INSPECTOR MALE
INSPECTOR FEMALE

Originally written for radio and transmitted on Radio 3 in April 1973, directed by Stewart Conn.

AUGUSTA	Jane Wymark
THOMAS	John Rowe
INSPECTOR I	Hugh Manning
INSPECTOR II	Ruth Goring

Adapted for the stage and performed at the Maximus Disco in October 1975.

AUGUSTA	Jill Dixon
THOMAS	Walter McMonagle
INSPECTOR I	Trevor Martin
INSPECTOR II	Ruth Goring

THE TWENTY-SECOND DAY

A room. There is a bed, a small table with a radio on it, a windowseat, one chair and a rug. The action takes place between THOMAS and AUGUSTA in the room and between the INSPECTORS and AUGUSTA in her imagination which can be designated by the shadowy periphery of the room or by lighting effects. It is necessary clearly to indicate Augusta's shifts between exterior and interior experience.

AUGUSTA is at the radio trying to tune into a station. Static, muffled police calls, whistling noises, snatches of foreign languages, etc.

AUGUSTA *(frightened. Switching radio off).*   Oh God!
THOMAS *(entering the room).*   Hello.
AUGUSTA.   Oh! It's you!
THOMAS.   Yes. Why are you surprised!
AUGUSTA.   Well I . . .
THOMAS.   Well you what?
AUGUSTA.   I . . . I . . .
THOMAS.   You didn't think I'd come back. *(She doesn't answer.)* Did you?
AUGUSTA.   No! I mean . . . no, I didn't.
THOMAS.   I don't understand that, I really don't. What was that before I came in — the radio again?
AUGUSTA.   Yes. I was just trying . . . You told me to.
THOMAS.   Ha! So you did think I was coming back.
AUGUSTA.   No. It just seemed . . . I mean I thought I would try some of the things you told me . . . the other time.
THOMAS *(pleased).*   Good. That's good. What happened?
AUGUSTA.   It was just the same.
THOMAS.   Nothing?
AUGUSTA.   Nothing that I could understand. You told me . . .
THOMAS.   What?
AUGUSTA.   You did. You told me it was easy.
THOMAS.   No. I didn't say easy. I said simple.
AUGUSTA *(sad).*   Yes.
THOMAS.   Never mind. I'll do it, shall I?
AUGUSTA.   Oh yes.

THOMAS. Okay. What would you like? Quiz programme? News? Music? A play?

AUGUSTA. Music. Please.

THOMAS. Right. Say no more. *(Switches on radio and tunes into music)* There. Yes?

AUGUSTA *(peaceful)*. Yes.

THOMAS *(sitting on bed)*. Come and sit here. Come on. Sit by me and I'll hold your hand.

AUGUSTA. All right.

THOMAS. You want to watch that, mate. You want to be very careful. You smiled then. Look out — you're doing it again. Might become a habit that. *(As she sits by him)* Give us your hand then. There. That nice?

AUGUSTA. Yes thank you.

THOMAS. You're very polite, aren't you? Are you always polite like that?

AUGUSTA *(troubled)*. I don't know.

THOMAS. Never mind. Doesn't matter. I can't think what to call you. Is that really your name — Augusta?

AUGUSTA *(surprised)*. Yes.

THOMAS. Bit of a mouthful. Why'd they call you that?

AUGUSTA. I was born in August.

THOMAS. So what? I was born in November. You know anybody called November?

AUGUSTA. No.

THOMAS. You laughed! Say my name.

AUGUSTA. Oh please . . .

THOMAS. Go on. Just say it.

AUGUSTA *(after a pause)*. Thomas.

THOMAS *(gently)*. See? That was simple.

AUGUSTA *(peaceful again)*. Yes.

Bring up music and then cut abruptly to silence.

INSPECTOR FEMALE. You say you sat next to each other.

AUGUSTA. Yes.

INSPECTOR MALE. And you had a conversation — an exchange of words?

AUGUSTA. Yes.

INSPECTOR FEMALE. Have we any corroboration concerning this event? Any evidence?

INSPECTOR MALE. Was there a transcript made?

AUGUSTA. A what?

INSPECTOR FEMALE. Any written proof. Did you take notes?

AUGUSTA. There was a note. I . . . I lost it.

INSPECTOR MALE. What did it say?

AUGUSTA. It said . . . I'll be back. Don't . . . don't forget Marmaduke.

INSPECTOR FEMALE. Meaningless. Unacceptable!

INSPECTOR MALE. Marmaduke . . .

THOMAS. Marmaduke's natural abilities and magnificent memory enabled him not only to master with ease those labyrinthine mazes of

English autography which so frequently perplex and bewilder the aspiring student, but also to answer successfully and fluently all the interminable and inconsistent series of arguments launched at him with persistent and exasperating re-iteration by litigious pettifoggers and literary critics inebriated by the exuberance of their own verbosity. *(Panting)* You have to say it all in one breath.

AUGUSTA. Why? What does it mean?

THOMAS. Dunno. It's an exercise I learned in acting classes. Breath control.

AUGUSTA *(polite)*. Oh. You're an actor.

THOMAS. No. I was going to be but I gave it up. I wasn't very good.

AUGUSTA. I'm sure you were.

THOMAS. You're doing it again.

AUGUSTA. Doing what?

THOMAS. Being polite. What's the point? I mean how could you be so sure of a thing like that? You don't know me. Do you?

AUGUSTA. No. *(Pause)* I'm sorry.

THOMAS. Don't do that. There's no need to be sorry. When you say things like that you're like someone going out of a room backwards — bowing.

AUGUSTA *(nervous)*. I don't know what you mean.

THOMAS. I mean I'd like you to be with me. Me personally. I don't want you to say things that you think I want to hear. I'm not a slot machine or an examination paper or something. You'll never get to know me that way — it's just putting me off.

AUGUSTA. I . . . I think . . . I expect it's . . . it's a habit.

THOMAS. No doubt, no doubt. Well it's a bad habit. Nasty. Far better off biting your nails or picking your nose. (AUGUSTA *just laughs again. Pleased.)* There you go. Now then. Do you want to know me?

AUGUSTA *(after a pause)*. Yes.

THOMAS. Good. Well I'm not an actor. I'm a lorry driver.

AUGUSTA. Oh — that must be very interesting.

THOMAS. Jesus! How fascinating it must be to be a lorry driver Mister whatever-your-name-is. Gracious. You must travel all over the country. I expect you get frightfully lonely sometimes don't you, Mr Thing? And I can't imagine how you handle those big heavy trucks. You must —

AUGUSTA. Wait. I didn't mean that. Really.

THOMAS. You didn't **mean** anything. Don't look so upset. We'll kick this thing together, Buster, count on me. Let's listen to something on the radio. I'll hold one of your hands and you can pick your nose with the other one. (AUGUSTA *really laughs. Tuning radio)* That is a very nice noise that laugh, I'll tell you. Now. What's this?

WOMAN *(on radio. Speaking over very delicate music. Heavily accented voice)*. This is my place. Look. Look. Such pretty little flowers. No weeds grow here. Columbines and violets and daisies and sweet scented roses without any thorns. Can you hear the birds? Little soft creatures chirping and twittering. Such a gentle noise. And the doves cooing, the breeze making the ferns whisper. So peaceful no? *(Cut music)* No. *(Her voice hardens)* Come in. Push past the flowers and the ferns, the little feathery birds. Now! *(Bring in dissonant note and hold it under rest of speech. Her voice grows more and more brutal as she goes on and the volume increases to very loud)* This is my place. This circle of burnt out ground. Charred black dead earth. And in the centre — look! There I am! The cobra's head, bright eyes, flickering tongue — the wrinkled fleshy neck of the vulture and the bulky wings. The thick stumpy ape's legs covered in fur — matted and foul with my own ordure. Look! Crouched. Waiting. Watching. Hungry. Now I rise. I flap my heavy wings. My tongue darts hatred. My claws scratch the dry earth as I move. I move . . .

AUGUSTA. Turn it off! Turn it off! *(Silence.)*

INSPECTOR FEMALE. Turn what off?

AUGUSTA *(panting)*. The radio. I don't want to hear it.

INSPECTOR MALE. There is no radio here. Please continue. You were telling us about yourself.

AUGUSTA. No! I wasn't!

INSPECTOR FEMALE. Of course you were. You said you were crouched . . .

AUGUSTA. No no no!

INSPECTOR FEMALE. And hungry . . .

AUGUSTA. Not angry no!

INSPECTOR FEMALE. I said 'hungry'.

INSPECTOR MALE. Was it hunger or anger? This is not clear.

AUGUSTA. I don't understand. I didn't say anything. It wasn't me.

INSPECTOR FEMALE *(genial)*. Well the words came from your direction and it sounded like your voice. What are you — a ventriloquist's dummy? *(The* INSPECTORS *laugh indulgently together.)*

INSPECTOR MALE *(stern)*. We are not making progress. This should not be difficult. We are simply trying to collect together a body of data — no matter how small — about the habitation of the room.

INSPECTOR FEMALE. And the genuine existence of the . . . visitor.

INSPECTOR MALE. Of course. You have been in the room for some time?

AUGUSTA. Yes.

INSPECTOR MALE. How long?

AUGUSTA. I don't know. *(The* INSPECTORS *whisper angrily to each other. Over them)* A long time! *(They stop)* As long as I can remember.

INSPECTOR FEMALE *(brisk)*. And you say you are frightened all of the time?

AUGUSTA. Most of the time.

INSPECTOR MALE. You are not frightened when the . . . visitor is present?

AUGUSTA. No.

INSPECTOR MALE. Mmmmm. And you see no other people at all?

AUGUSTA. Well I see them. There's a window in the room. I watch the street below and all the people down there.

INSPECTOR FEMALE. You say you look down on them? You feel contempt?

AUGUSTA. No I didn't mean that. The room is very high up in the building.

INSPECTOR MALE. What do you feel about them?

AUGUSTA *(too quickly)*. Nothing really. I just watch. *(The*
INSPECTORS *whisper together again. Over them)* Envy. I feel envy
and . . . and fear too.

INSPECTOR MALE. Why?

AUGUSTA. They all look as if they're doing something — as if they
know what they're doing. They look . . . busy and strong. Buying things,
going places . . . talking to each other. And . . .

INSPECTOR FEMALE. And?

AUGUSTA *(rapidly)*. There are so many old people — very old. *(To*
herself. Troubled) I can't understand it. What makes them stay alive so
long? Why do they want to? How do they survive.

INSPECTOR MALE *(jolly)*. I expect you think they should all be killed
off, eh?

AUGUSTA. No. No.

INSPECTOR FEMALE. All the old and the weak?

AUGUSTA. No! Not them. Not **them.**

INSPECTOR MALE *(hard)*. Who then? *(She doesn't answer.)*

INSPECTOR FEMALE *(coldly)*. I suggest we abandon this enquiry.

INSPECTOR MALE. Not allowed. As you know it is clearly stated: as
long as there is one to answer the questions, the questions must be asked.

INSPECTOR FEMALE. But we are getting no answers. Impertinence,
evasion . . . probably lies.

INSPECTOR MALE. Please. Let me explain. Once proceedings such as
these are set in motion, once they are begun —

AUGUSTA *(frightened but insistent)*. How begun? Who began?

INSPECTOR FEMALE *(cordially unpleasant)*. You spoke?

AUGUSTA *(stronger)*. I need to know. How did this begin?

INSPECTOR MALE *(patient)*. Have we the first meeting recorded?

INSPECTOR FEMALE. Certainly.

INSPECTOR MALE. Let us hear it please.

The following is recorded

INSPECTOR MALE. Will the accused rise.

INSPECTOR FEMALE. Self-accused.

INSPECTOR MALE. I stand corrected. You are fully aware of the
reasons for which you are here.

AUGUSTA *(tired)*. Yes.

INSPECTOR MALE. You claim no external pressures?

AUGUSTA. No.

INSPECTOR FEMALE. You have freely and in full knowledge applied
for solitary confinement?

AUGUSTA. Yes.

INSPECTOR MALE. And you wish no mitigating circumstances to be
brought forward?

AUGUSTA. No.

INSPECTOR FEMALE. Nor to beg leniency at this time or during the
subsequent proceedings?

AUGUSTA. No.

INSPECTOR MALE.   We will now proceed to your confession. You are
  required to enumerate those counts on which you—
THOMAS *(switching off the radio)*.   Bloody pretentious rubbish. Sorry.
  Did you really want to hear it?
AUGUSTA *(confused)*.   What?
THOMAS.   You said you wanted to hear how it began.
AUGUSTA.   I said that to you?
THOMAS.   Well. You said it. And I'm the only one here besides you—
  as far as I know. Or have you got another man hidden here? Ha! Do I see
  you blush? So that's it—you're betraying me with another man aren't
  you? You—
AUGUSTA.   No! Honestly.
THOMAS *(sad)*.   Always so serious.
AUGUSTA.   I'm sorry.
THOMAS.   Don't apologise.
AUGUSTA.   I—
THOMAS.   And don't apologise for apologising. Now. Do you want the
  radio on again?
AUGUSTA.   What was it about?
THOMAS.   I dunno. Some play about a political prisoner. I don't mind
  listening if you want to.
AUGUSTA.   No. I wasn't really listening. I was . . . I thought . . .
THOMAS.   Yes?
AUGUSTA.   Nothing.
THOMAS *(after a pause)*.   What happened to that rose I brought you?
AUGUSTA.   Oh . . . it . . . *(hastily)* It died.
THOMAS *(mild)*.   It flaming didn't.
AUGUSTA.   No. That was a lie. I lost it.
THOMAS *(gently)*.   You're always lying and you're always losing things.
AUGUSTA *(sad)*.   Yes.
THOMAS.   Why?
AUGUSTA.   I . . . I . . . Sometimes the room seems so full that I don't
  know how I should look for anything and then . . . other times . . . it's so
  empty there doesn't seem to be anything to find . . . That's true. That
  isn't a lie.
THOMAS.   I know. Never mind, never mind. *(Brisk)* Well if we're not
  going to listen to the radio—you tell me a story.
AUGUSTA *(astonished)*.   I can't.
THOMAS.   Yes, you can, yes you can. Anybody can tell a story. Doesn't
  matter what it's about.
AUGUSTA.   But I don't know how.
THOMAS.   Try.
AUGUSTA.   But there's nothing . . . you see I don't . . . I *(she takes a
  breath. Then factually)* Once there was a little old woman who lived in a
  cave in a forest. She was very gnarled and humped and if anybody walked
  through the wood where she was she would just stand still and they would
  take her for some kind of bush or a little dead tree. She used to sit out in
  front of her cave at night smoking a pipe and howling like a dog.
THOMAS *(after a pause)*.   What happened to her?
AUGUSTA.   Nothing. That's all.

THOMAS *(after another pause).*   Do you know how long you've been in this room?
AUGUSTA *(surprised).*   I told them. A long time.
THOMAS.   Who's them?
AUGUSTA *(quickly).*   No one. No one.

There is a click and the following is recorded.

AUGUSTA.   . . . little dead tree. She used to sit out in front of her cave at night smoking a pipe and howling like a dog.
THOMAS.   What happened to her?
AUGUSTA.   Nothing. That's all.
THOMAS.   Do you know how long you've been in this room?
AUGUSTA.   I told them.

And the recording clicks off.

INSPECTOR FEMALE *(harsh).*   You have spoken about us.
INSPECTOR MALE.   You know that is forbidden.
AUGUSTA.   It was a mistake. It was just a mistake. But I told him there was no one.
INSPECTOR FEMALE.   Still. He will be curious. *(Sharp)* Who is he?
AUGUSTA.   I don't know.
INSPECTOR MALE.   Where does he come from? How long have you known him?
AUGUSTA.   I don't know. I don't know.
INSPECTOR FEMALE *(somewhat nagging tone).*   You spend hours with this . . . person. Alone with him. And we know nothing whatever about him. You say he is virtually a stranger to you and yet you call him by his first name. You hold hands with him. *(Very unpleasant low laughter from INSPECTOR MALE.)*
INSPECTOR MALE *(recovering himself. Pompous).*   We must ask you not to see him again. We must insist. We have that right. It is for your own good.
THOMAS.   Augusta.
INSPECTOR FEMALE *(swift).*   Don't answer. We are only thinking of you.
INSPECTOR MALE.   Apart from which the room itself is dangerous. The cracks between the floorboards are wide enough to fall through.
INSPECTOR FEMALE.   Underneath the rug there is a gaping hole with deep water below.
INSPECTOR MALE.   The walls bulge. They could fall on you while you were sleeping.
INSPECTOR FEMALE.   Suffocate you.
THOMAS.   Augusta.
INSPECTOR MALE.   Don't let him in. You're safe here.
INSPECTOR FEMALE.   He is keeping you a prisoner in the room.
AUGUSTA.   No. No. He's kind. He brings me food.
INSPECTOR FEMALE *(snort of laughter).*   So do jailors.
INSPECTOR MALE.   You have said that sometimes the room is full. Full of what?

AUGUSTA. It's nothing. Nothing. I said it seems full. Sometimes I think I see things but it isn't —

INSPECTOR FEMALE. What things?

AUGUSTA. He says I imagine them.

INSPECTOR MALE. Of course he does. He would say that. *(Kind)* Don't you understand? We're trying to protect you.

INSPECTOR FEMALE *(gentle)*. Tell us what you see. We want to help you.

AUGUSTA. They are only . . . they are like dreams except I'm awake. Sometimes it's people. There was a street corner in the room . . . not in the room. A foreign city and people walking rapidly past me. Ordinary people with very familar faces. But one or two of them in the crowd were like people in a negative — glaring white eyes, gleaming teeth and smoky black faces. Then there was a staircase in the room . . . not in the room. An old palace — Italian I think. Women are moving slowly down one side of the stairs in silk and velvet gowns. *(Her voice takes on a lingering dreamy quality and the* INSPECTORS *make little murmurs of contentment at intervals)* The men move down the other side of the stairs. Heavy, ponderous, important men. Judges and kings in robes and jewels. The light on the staircase is gloomy and soft and gold. It is a silent solemn time. Peaceful. And then as they come closer towards me *(accelerates)* I see that their heads are soft . . . monstrous! Lupus heads! *(Terror. Breathless)* Wolves and lions — misshapen swollen blind!

INSPECTOR FEMALE *(after a pause)*. What else do you see?

AUGUSTA *(somewhat childlike)*. Sometimes I am in the sky in the room . . . not in the room. Looking down into the tops of trees. Great big trees with a million leaves all dark green and shiny and rustling and rushing like a river below. And there are swans! Swimming in the tops of the trees. And once I was looking down into a field in the room . . . not in the room. A long, long way down and the grass was soft and rich. Beautiful. And then I saw a little white ferret running and running across the field. Just a tiny sleek little white ferret but it was frightened and running so fast. And then I wasn't looking a long way down but I was closer and it wasn't . . . *(she begins to stammer. As she goes on she starts to weep)* a ferret . . . it wasn't . . . it was a . . . it's a girl . . ! it's a white naked girl. She's running . . . she's afraid . . . you can see . . . naked! naked!

Blackout and the sound of a slap. AUGUSTA *cries out. A long cry. Then lights up in the room.*

AUGUSTA *(to* THOMAS. *Puzzled)*. You hurt me.

THOMAS. I'm sorry. I didn't know what to do. I speak to you but you don't hear me. You're like a statue. You just sit there staring.

AUGUSTA *(abruptly)*. This room is dangerous.

THOMAS. Eh? What do you mean — dangerous?

AUGUSTA. The cracks in the floor are too wide. You could fall through them. There's a hole under the rug.

THOMAS *(incredulous)*. What?

AUGUSTA. There is. And there's water below and it's deep and dirty and cold!

THOMAS. Oh look. Come on. There isn't any hole under the rug. Look.
I'll show you.

AUGUSTA. Don't touch it!

THOMAS. All right. All right.

AUGUSTA *(busy. Planning. To herself)*. I'll sit over here. On the
windowseat. Yes. Yes. This will be all right. If I keep my feet off the
floor. It will be all right like this.

THOMAS *(under his breath)*. Oh Christ. *(Then too brightly to her)* You
look like a bird perching on a telephone wire. *(She doesn't answer)*
Augusta. Look at me. That's it. Listen. You know there aren't any holes
in the floor, don't you. You know that.

AUGUSTA *(rapid)*. Be careful. I should be careful. You're standing
very near to one of the cracks.

THOMAS. Right. Now watch! *(He jumps on the floor)*.

AUGUSTA. Don't.

THOMAS *(punctuating speech with jumps)*. Watch me! Watch me! I'm
jumping on every single crack. There! And again! This is a lovely strong
floor, Missis, believe me. Bam! And once more. Step on a crack. Break
your mother's back. And now *(gets up on chair)* for a quick plunge into
the swimming pool under the rug. One . . . two . . .

AUGUSTA. Oh don't don't please don't.

THOMAS *(landing on rug)*. Three! Blow me where's the water? I come
out for a swim and they whip the pool away behind my back. Let's have a
look under this rug. Now then. Alley oop. Bloody disappeared. There's
nothing under this rug but floor. What a liberty. *(There is a pause. Then
gently to her)* Well? What do you think?

AUGUSTA. I don't know. I don't know.

THOMAS *(going to her)*. Well I'll tell you. What it is, mate, is that you
have got a bit mixed up again about what's real and what you imagine in
your head. What you suffer from, my dear Watson, is a touch of the old
hallucinations.

AUGUSTA *(slowly)*. He told me that . . .

THOMAS *(carefully)*. Who did?

AUGUSTA. He was behind a . . . a desk? They asked him . . .

THOMAS. Who asked him?

AUGUSTA. I . . . I . . . I don't remember. *(Looks at him, puzzled)*
Were you there?

THOMAS. You tell me, Augusta. Was I there?

AUGUSTA *(precipitant)*. There's the walls too. They're bulging and
crumbling. They could easily fall in and suffocate me while I'm asleep.

THOMAS *(sighs. Then cheerful)*. Walls is it? Charlie will you just check
those walls for the lady? *(In another silly voice as he moves over to the
walls and thumps them)* Righto cock, leave it to me. Nothing the matter
with these walls, mate. Lovely set of walls this. No chance of these falling
down. You'd have to set off a bomb to get these down. *(Reluctantly
AUGUSTA laughs)*. There you go. That's all right then. *(Goes to her)*
Do you know why you thought all that? About the floor and the walls and
under the rug and all?

AUGUSTA. No.

THOMAS.   Well now you know it's okay you can come down off of the
telephone wire, eh? Here. I'll help you. That's it. All right?

AUGUSTA *(exhausted)*.   Yes.

THOMAS.   Tell you what. Let's tuck you up in your bed. I'll go and get us
something to eat and you can listen to the afternoon story on the radio.
Would you like that?

AUGUSTA.   Yes.

THOMAS.   Say no more. Here. *(Lifts her and carries her to the bed)*
Shoes off I think. And we'll pull up the eiderdown. That's the way.
Comfortable?

AUGUSTA.   Yes

THOMAS.   Right. Now then . . . *(goes to radio and tunes it)*

RADIO *(man's voice)*.   It was late afternoon. The huge grey building
seemed sullen and empty. The last rays of sunlight caught the rows of
windows making them look like hundreds of dazzled, angry eyes. From
time to time there was the muffled sound of secret hurrying footsteps in
some distant corridor. The drone of a passing jet swelled and tore the
silent sky.

THOMAS *(who has been putting on his coat)*.   I'll be back soon. Okay?
(Says this over the last couple of sentences of the above.)

AUGUSTA.   Yes. *(He goes.)*

RADIO.   The door closed behind him. He stood in the hall rigid and
listening. Nothing. He knelt on the floor and pressed his ear against the
door, his face sharp with concentration. Not a sound. With great care he
rose to his feet and began to tiptoe toward the stairs, but as his hand
grasped the bannister he was seized by an overwhelming desire to laugh.
*(This speech increases gradually in volume and she raises herself slowly to
a sitting posture on the bed staring at the radio.)* He clapped his hand over
his mouth. Helpless he doubled up, shaking with silent hilarity. It had
been so simple, so stupidly amazingly simple. A primitive juggling trick
with reality — the crudest kind of legerdemain. Like hypnotising a baby
rabbit. He rocked and swayed at the top of the stairs, his face contorted.
He took a long breath. He must control himself. There was a great deal
to do. He straightened and brushed the tears of laughter from his cheeks.
He began to move slowly, carefully down the stairs. As he reached the
front door his foot brushed against some empty milk bottles. There was a
little chink of glass. *(Sound of chink from distance.)* She sat bolt upright
her eyes staring. That noise! *(Chink of glass closer)*. She pushed herself
wildly back against the wall. The fierce blind terror devoured her. *(Very
loud sound of breaking glass)*

INSPECTOR FEMALE.   And now you know.

AUGUSTA *(panting)*.   Yes.

INSPECTOR MALE.   We tried to warn you. You wouldn't listen to us.

AUGUSTA.   Yes . . . yes.

INSPECTOR FEMALE.   He is your enemy. He was always your enemy.

INSPECTOR MALE.   He has followed you everywhere but you never
recognised him.

INSPECTOR FEMALE.   Watching. Waiting to make you his captive. To
destroy you.

AUGUSTA *(pleading)*.   No no no no no.

INSPECTOR MALE. Yes! He was the one behind the desk. Don't you remember?

AUGUSTA. I can't be sure. I'm not sure. He didn't look the same.

INSPECTOR FEMALE *(short laugh)*. He never looks the same. He can take any face he chooses.

INSPECTOR MALE. Don't you believe us?

AUGUSTA. I don't want to. I don't want to.

INSPECTOR FEMALE. Do you remember what happened to the little old woman?

AUGUSTA. Yes. I remember.

INSPECTOR MALE. Tell us.

AUGUSTA. They came to the forest where she was sitting outside her cave. They took her away from the shadows and the quiet. It was all quick and noisy. They put her in a car and the buildings rushed past and there were bells and roars and crashing and someone sobbing in the car and the white burning sky tipped and slanted up above.

INSPECTOR MALE. Go on.

AUGUSTA. They took her to the place.

INSPECTOR FEMALE. And?

AUGUSTA. They brought her into a room. They tried to make her sit down but she wouldn't. She stood like a dead tree in the middle of the floor. They talked and talked and talked. They asked her questions but she didn't answer them. Once she howled like a dog.

INSPECTOR MALE. And then?

AUGUSTA. And then they left her there in the room alone with the man behind the desk.

INSPECTOR FEMALE. Him!

INSPECTOR MALE. And now he has you prisoner!

AUGUSTA. No. Wait. Wait. **He** was in a different room — in the high part of the place. *(Remembering. Stronger)* Corridors and lifts and then there is a big room with tables. Food. And people sitting and eating. The little old woman sits at a table but she doesn't eat. Then **he** comes. He sits next to her. The one behind the desk is gone. Left far below in the first room. This one doesn't ask her any questions. He looks into her terrible eyes and smiles. Not afraid. He talks to her and feeds her soup and little bits of bread the way you would feed a bird. The days go by and by and he is always sitting next to her feeding her like a bird.

INSPECTOR FEMALE *(urgent)*. It is the same one! Listen! It is always the same one. The enemy! Do you remember the old man with the yellow face who crawled along the corridor in the night crying and spitting?

INSPECTOR MALE. The tall man in the garden who leaned on his broom and stared and stared?

INSPECTOR FEMALE. The boy who laughed?

INSPECTOR MALE. Disguises.

INSPECTOR FEMALE. It was always he.

AUGUSTA. I don't understand. I don't understand.

INSPECTOR MALE *(busy lecturing tone)*. It isn't at all difficult to understand. Simply concentrate. We've said all this to you before.

INSPECTOR FEMALE *(rueful mother)*. You don't listen.

INSPECTOR MALE.   And it's no use pretending to us that you're
stupid. That's just a silly waste of time.
INSPECTOR FEMALE.   Not stupid — stubborn!
INSPECTOR MALE.   Now. Once more. I'll explain it to you one more
time.
INSPECTOR FEMALE.   Try and pay attention.
INSPECTOR MALE *(sighs. Clears his throat).*   Among the millions that
are born to cover the earth there have always been some who are
marked. The mark of the victim. And for each victim there is,
somewhere, an enemy. No one can see the mark of the victim except the
enemy. The enemy knows from the beginning that he is an enemy. The
victim does not know he is a victim until the first time he meets his
enemy's eyes. From that moment all the victim's power and passion must
be spent on evading the enemy. Through his mark, his crucial wound, the
enemy will pierce him and destroy him. The victim knows now, and it is
the only thing he can afford to know, that he is the prey to the hunter
enemy. If he is not to perish he must flee. Forever now he must be
watchful, alert to his fearful danger. Behind any face, inside any body the
hunter may be hidden. There is no safety. No one to trust. His single task
now is to escape. *(The room begins to dim and* AUGUSTA *begins to
slowly curl herself up into a foetal position on the bed.)* And the way of
escape is withdrawal — retreat into his own inner world. There the
enemy cannot penetrate, cannot reach him. Enclosed in his grey,
internal silence he is invulnerable. No movement must be made toward
any other living creature lest he be the enemy. No greetings exchanged,
no bonds forged. This is the only way. (THOMAS *enters.*)
RADIO *(man's voice as before).*   The old schoolteacher got up from her
chair by the window. The room was nearly dark. Once again a jet plane
passed over the silent building and the sky was cracked by the roar. As
she reached the door the sound died away and she spoke once more in
her dry kind voice. 'Remember what I have told you. There is a perverse
and dreadful accuracy in us all which can make us select the exact person
who is most dangerous to us. Othello and Iago — victim and enemy
partnered in the inexorable tragic dance. Remember. You are safe now.
Try and understand. Try and forgive.' And she was gone. *(Announcer's
voice)* You have been listening to the Afternoon Story, 'Prison Visitor'
by —
THOMAS *(turning off the radio).*   Prison Visitor eh? Sounds a bit grim.
What was it like?
AUGUSTA *(tense).*   I don't know.
THOMAS.   It's getting dark in here. I'll turn on the lamp. Why? Did you
fall asleep?
AUGUSTA.   I don't know.
THOMAS *(turns on the lamp. Turns to her. Trying not to show too much
alarm).*   What's up? *(Goes to her)* Never mind. Never mind. It doesn't
matter. Here — give us your hand.
AUGUSTA *(violently).*   Don't!
THOMAS *(after a pause).*   Do you know something? It's the
twenty-second day today. Twenty-two days. *(After waiting for her to
answer)* I've brought some hot chocolate and some sandwiches. Here.
Have a bit of this. Open your mouth.

AUGUSTA. No!

THOMAS. Not hungry?

AUGUSTA *(fierce)*. I don't want you to feed me!

THOMAS *(another pause. Then determinedly cheerful)*. Right. I'll put them down here by the bed while I have mine. Must say I didn't think much of the sound of that story. *(Begins to eat sandwich)* Think I might have fallen asleep myself. That's rubbish — all that about victims and enemies. Well not rubbish maybe, but wrong. Except for that bit about people choosing just the wrong person. Funny business altogether that. You see it all the time in marriage. Top notch sandwiches these. Try some?

AUGUSTA. No!

THOMAS *(looks at her. Then continues with some effort)*. I mean, a person has some weakness — some sort of silly, wrong part of themselves that has got mixed up inside them. Nine times out of ten they'll go out and get married to just the kind of person who'll make the wrong part wronger. Know what I mean? Puts you off the idea of marriage a bit, that one. Still, you couldn't say either person was the victim **or** the enemy. They're both if you follow me. To each other. For example, take Othello and Iago, like she said. After all they both came to a sticky end. If you look at it one way Iago's the victim. If old Othello hadn't listened to all the wrong voices inside himself that told him all those lies were true, Iago probably would have settled down all right and —

AUGUSTA. Voices?

THOMAS. What? *(She has uncurled herself and is up on one elbow)* Oh. Yeah. You know what I mean. *(Goes to her)* Like — tell you something funny . . . well, sad really when you come to think about it. Ever since I was a kid, whenever I'm happy — really having a good time, you know? Well all of a sudden there's this voice inside me says 'Yes, but what **should** you be doing?'.

AUGUSTA *(quickly)*. What does it sound like?

THOMAS. Dunno. Never really thought about it. I suppose it sounded like whoever it was that was screwing me up at the time. You know. Like the matron in the orphanage. I ever tell you I was an orphan? No mother no father. *(Looks at her. Gentle)* Go on. Have just a little bit of sandwich. *(She opens her mouth and he feeds her)* There you go. Good isn't it? Have a bit more. Open your mouth again. That's right. Yeah, probably the matron. A real cow that woman. Then teachers — people like that, bosses, the welfare people — all sorts. 'Yes but what should you be doing?' Loud and clear. Do you want some of your chocolate? *(She gets up suddenly and crosses the room)* Where are you going?

AUGUSTA *(urgent)*. Come over here.

THOMAS *(crosses to her)*. All right.

AUGUSTA *(whispers)*. I think they're in the radio.

THOMAS. Who?

AUGUSTA. Shhh! They might be able to hear us.

THOMAS *(low)*. Who are they, Augusta? Tell me who they are.

AUGUSTA. They know things. They say things about you.

THOMAS. What? What things?

AUGUSTA. I can't tell you. I can't tell you. They may be listening.

THOMAS *(looks at her for a moment. Then firm)*.   Let's go out.

AUGUSTA *(astonished)*.   Out?

THOMAS.   Yes. Out of this room.

AUGUSTA.   I can't go out of here.

THOMAS.   Why not?

AUGUSTA.   Because I've always been here.

THOMAS.   No.

AUGUSTA.   I can't get out. I'm supposed to stay here.

THOMAS.   You can. Try. You haven't tried. You haven't always been here. I promise you.

AUGUSTA.   I don't know if I can believe you. I don't know who to believe.

THOMAS.   Here — come to the window. *(They cross to the windowseat behind which the INSPECTORS stand side-by-side. As THOMAS speaks they separate and draw away.)* Look over there. See? That's my lorry. Just across the street. We'll go through this door. You can, Augusta. And we'll go out of the building and just cross the street and climb up into the lorry. You'll like it. It's little and warm in there. Safe. And you sit so high up you can see everything. We'll drive right out of the town into the country. It's simple to leave this room, you'll see.

AUGUSTA *(staring out of the window. Very intent)*.   Are you sure?

THOMAS.   Sure. You can go anywhere, Augusta. You don't have to stay in this place. I'll take you away.

AUGUSTA *(frightened. She crouches suddenly down on the floor)*.   Oh God!

THOMAS.   What is it? Augusta what's wrong?

AUGUSTA *(shivers and hugs herself as if very cold)*.   You said that before. You said that. I can remember.

And silently INSPECTORS *leave the stage.*

THOMAS *(crouches down beside her. Speaks with great care)*.   What can you remember, Augusta. Tell me.

AUGUSTA *(rises and so does THOMAS. They look at each other as she speaks)*.   The place. The place. You took me away from the place. I found you in the garden. You'd left me, hadn't you? You'd gone away from me.

THOMAS.   Yes. Forgive me.

AUGUSTA.   But you came back. While you were gone the . . . the old . . . the little old woman . . . She wouldn't talk to any of them. She tried . . . I . . . I tried to get back to the forest . . . They came back . . . the ones. Looking and staring . . . talking and talking and talking but she . . . I . . . I wouldn't look at them. Afraid . . . afraid of them. The woman . . . my . . . my . . . the woman cried and the man . . . my . . . my . . . he tried to touch me. He tried to put his arms around me. *(Cries)* I couldn't, Thomas, I couldn't!

THOMAS.   No. Don't cry, dear heart, don't cry.

AUGUSTA *(exhausted)*.   No. I can see. I can see. Before the forest . . . before I went away from them . . .

THOMAS.   Yes?